T0219707

Lecture Notes in Computer Science 9390

Commenced Publication in 1973
Founding and Former Series Editors:
Gerhard Goos, Juris Hartmanis, and Jan van Leeuwen

More information about this series at http://www.springer.com/series/7410

Sjouke Mauw · Barbara Kordy
Sushil Jajodia (Eds.)

Graphical Models for Security

Second International Workshop, GraMSec 2015
Verona, Italy, July 13, 2015
Revised Selected Papers

 Springer

Editors
Sjouke Mauw
University of Luxembourg
Luxembourg
Luxembourg

Sushil Jajodia
George Mason University
Fairfax, VA
USA

Barbara Kordy
INSA Rennes and IRISA
Rennes
France

ISSN 0302-9743   ISSN 1611-3349 (electronic)
Lecture Notes in Computer Science
ISBN 978-3-319-29967-9   ISBN 978-3-319-29968-6 (eBook)
DOI 10.1007/978-3-319-29968-6

Library of Congress Control Number: 2016931195

LNCS Sublibrary: SL4 – Security and Cryptology

Printed on acid-free paper

This Springer imprint is published by SpringerNature
The registered company is Springer International Publishing AG Switzerland

Preface

The present volume contains the proceedings of the Second International Workshop on Graphical Models for Security (GraMSec 2015). The workshop was held in Verona, Italy, on July 13, 2015, in conjunction with the 28th IEEE Computer Security Foundations Symposium (CSF 2015).

Graphical security models provide an intuitive but systematic methodology to analyze security weaknesses of systems and to evaluate potential protection measures. Formal methods and computer security researchers, as well as security professionals from industry and government, have proposed various graphical security modeling schemes. Such models are used to capture different security facets (digital, physical, and social) and address a range of challenges including security assessment, risk analysis, automated defensing, secure services composition, policy validation, and verification.

The objective of the International Workshop on Graphical Models for Security is to contribute to the development of well-founded graphical security models, efficient algorithms for their analysis, as well as methodologies for their practical usage. The workshop brings together academic researchers and industry practitioners designing and employing visual models for security in order to provide a platform for discussion, knowledge exchange, and collaborations.

The second edition of the GraMSec workshop received 13 submissions and each of them was reviewed by at least four reviewers. Based on their quality and contribution to the field, six papers, among which one short tool paper, were accepted for presentation at the workshop and inclusion in the final proceedings of GraMSec 2015. In addition to the accepted papers, we invited Christian Probst, Jan Willemson, and Wolter Pieters from the TREsPASS consortium to describe the Attack Navigator, a graphical approach to security risk assessment inspired by navigation systems. The workshop's program was complemented by an invited lecture by Marc Bouissou on "Dynamic Graphical Models for Security and Safety Joint Modeling."

We would like to thank all the people who volunteered their time and energy to make this year's workshop happen. In particular, we thank the authors for submitting their manuscripts to the workshop and all the attendees for contributing to the workshop discussions. We are also grateful to the members of the Program Committee and the external reviewers for their work in reviewing and discussing the submissions, and their commitment to meeting the strict deadlines. Further, we would like to thank Ravi Jhawar (publicity chair), Piotr Kordy (web chair), and Luca Viganò (General Chair of CSF 2015) for their support in organizing our workshop.

Finally, our thanks go to the European Commission's Seventh Framework Programme for their partial sponsorship of the workshop (EU FP7 grant no. 318003 TREsPASS) and to the University of Luxembourg, the Fonds National de la Recherche Luxembourg (FNR-CORE grant ADT2P), the Institut National des Sciences

Appliquées (INSA Rennes), and the Institut de Recherche en Informatique et Systèmes Aléatoires (IRISA) for their in kind contribution to GraMSec 2015.

July 2015

Sjouke Mauw
Barbara Kordy
Sushil Jajodia

Organization

Program Committee

Mathieu Acher	University Rennes 1 and IRISA, France
Massimiliano Albanese	George Mason University, USA
Ludovic Apvrille	Télécom ParisTech, France
Thomas Bauereiss	DFKI GmbH, Germany
Giampaolo Bella	University of Catania, Italy
Stefano Bistarelli	University of Perugia, Italy
Ahto Buldas	Cybernetica, Estonia
Jason Crampton	Royal Holloway University of London, UK
Frédéric Cuppens	Télécom Bretagne, France
Mathias Ekstedt	KTH Royal Institute of Technology, Sweden
Olga Gadyatskaya	University of Luxembourg, Luxembourg
Paolo Giorgini	University of Trento, Italy
Erlend Andreas Gjære	SINTEF, Norway
Dieter Gollmann	TU Hamburg-Harburg, Germany
Olivier Heen	Technicolor, France
Siv Hilde Houmb	Secure-NOK AS and Gjøvik University College, Norway
Sushil Jajodia	George Mason University, USA
Ravi Jhawar	University of Luxembourg, Luxembourg
Henk Jonkers	BiZZdesign, The Netherlands
Jan Jürjens	Technical University Dortmund, Germany
Dong Seong Kim	University of Canterbury, New Zealand
Barbara Kordy	INSA Rennes and IRISA, France
Jean-Louis Lanet	Inria, France
Gurvan Le Guernic	DGA Maîtrise de l'Information, France
Sjouke Mauw	University of Luxembourg, Luxembourg
Per Håkon Meland	SINTEF, Norway
Jogesh Muppala	HKUST, Hong Kong, SAR China
Flemming Nielson	Technical University of Denmark, Denmark
Steven Noel	MITRE and George Mason University, USA
Andreas L. Opdahl	University of Bergen, Norway
Stéphane Paul	Thales Research and Technology, France
Wolter Pieters	Delft University of Technology, The Netherlands
Sophie Pinchinat	University Rennes 1 and IRISA, France
Vincenzo Piuri	University of Milan, Italy
Ludovic Piètre-Cambacédès	EDF, France
Nicolas Prigent	Supélec, France

Cristian Prisacariu	University of Oslo, Norway
Christian W. Probst	Technical University of Denmark, Denmark
David Pym	University College London, UK
Saša Radomirović	ETH Zürich, Switzerland
Indrajit Ray	Colorado State University, USA
Arend Rensink	University of Twente, The Netherlands
Yves Roudier	EURECOM, France
Pierangela Samarati	University of Milan, Italy
Guttorm Sindre	Norwegian University of Science and Technology, Norway
Ketil Stølen	SINTEF and University of Oslo, Norway
Axel Tanner	IBM Research Zürich, Switzerland
Kishor S. Trivedi	Duke University, USA
Luca Viganò	King's College London, UK
Lingyu Wang	Concordia University, Canada
Jan Willemson	Cybernetica, Estonia

Additional Reviewers

Aslanyan, Zaruhi
Erdogan, Gencer
Ivanova, Marieta Georgieva
Pouly, Marc

Contents

The Attack Navigator

Christian W. Probst[1]([✉]), Jan Willemson[2], and Wolter Pieters[3]

[1] Technical University of Denmark, Kongens Lyngby, Denmark
cwpr@dtu.dk
[2] Cybernetica, Tallinn, Estonia
janwil@cyber.ee
[3] Delft University of Technology, Delft, The Netherlands
w.pieters@tudelft.nl

Abstract. The need to assess security and take protection decisions is at least as old as our civilisation. However, the complexity and development speed of our interconnected technical systems have surpassed our capacity to imagine and evaluate risk scenarios. This holds in particular for risks that are caused by the strategic behaviour of adversaries. Therefore, technology-supported methods are needed to help us identify and manage these risks. In this paper, we describe the attack navigator: a graph-based approach to security risk assessment inspired by navigation systems. Based on maps of a socio-technical system, the attack navigator identifies routes to an attacker goal. Specific attacker properties such as skill or resources can be included through attacker profiles. This enables defenders to explore attack scenarios and the effectiveness of defense alternatives under different threat conditions.

1 Introduction

The need to assess security and take protection decisions is as old as our civilisation, and maybe even older. Looking around in nature, we see that animals try to build their lairs in safe places and that some plants grow prickles. These kinds of decisions are not taken in a conscious way, but are rather a result of a long evolutionary trial and error process.

What differentiates humans from other species is the highly complex technical environment we operate in. The speed of development of this environment exceeds the capabilities of natural evolution by several orders of magnitude, which means we cannot rely on evolution to develop safeguards. Instead, we need security assessment methods to identify potential threats, and to allow us to cope with the highly sophisticated attacks being enabled by our environment.

On the other hand, our perception of surroundings is still very much limited by what evolution has provided for us. Humans are averagely good at perceiving visual images, sounds, and smells, but not so much at grasping all the small details and implications of large infrastructures. Yet, in order to utilize such infrastructures efficiently, we need such abilities in one way or another.

© Springer International Publishing Switzerland 2016
S. Mauw et al. (Eds.): GraMSec 2015, LNCS 9390, pp. 1–17, 2016.
DOI: 10.1007/978-3-319-29968-6_1

Even if humans manage to collect adequate environmental data, their risk comprehension may be severely biased due to educational, cultural, psychological, political, and other reasons [1–3]. Hence, there is a clear need for tools that provide a visual, easy to comprehend overview of the environment, but at the same time being rational and unambiguous. The target of the TRE$_S$PASS project [4] is to achieve exactly that – assist humans in taking security decisions about large, complex infrastructures in a way that is easy to perceive given our limited capabilities.

In security risks, we deal with strategic attackers who plan their actions. This means that we must be able to "think thief", and predict possible attack scenarios by imagining attacker behaviour. The central innovation to achieve this goal is the introduction of the notion of *attack navigator map*. It can be seen as an effort to bridge the gap between complexity of real systems and limits of human perception by utilising a concept familiar to all of us, namely spatial navigation. This approach gives us several benefits:

- Moving towards an attacker's goal corresponds intuitively well to navigating through complex terrain, together with the need to take decisions, achieve subgoals, etc.
- Navigation optimisation is rather well studied and understood, as opposed to complex system security.
- Navigation can be handled on different levels of abstraction. There can be a bird-eye version for executive-level, grass-root version for technical level, and an arbitrary number of intermediate levels as needed.

All these aspects make navigation a good metaphor for studying security assessment of complex infrastructures and for communicating assessment results.

The remainder of this paper is organised as follows. In Sect. 2 we outline the main steps of the TRE$_S$PASS process that provides analysts with the toolset and methodology forming the basis of the attack navigator, which then is described in Sect. 3. Sections 4 and 5 explain how to move from a high-level abstract view of the environment (the satellite view) to a fine-grained system model (the map) and how to find routes (the attacks). Finally, Sect. 6 discusses how to select countermeasures based on TRE$_S$PASS analysis, and Sect. 7 draws some conclusions.

2   The TRE$_S$PASS Process

Of course it takes more than just a good metaphor to build a usable risk assessment system. In practice, the analyst needs a working toolset and methodology that would be able to support the navigation approach on various levels of abstraction. The main result of the TRE$_S$PASS project are the toolset and methodology that together support the TRE$_S$PASS process, which we describe in this section.

In order to achieve the navigation effect, one needs an analogue of a map to navigate on. In the real world, maps represent cities and streets, and to a certain extent artefacts such as points of interest. These maps are produced by geographers based on satellite images and inspection of the terrain under consideration. In the TRE$_S$PASS approach, the role of a map is played by the *system model*, a formal representation of the socio-technical environment to be analysed. System models contain a number of components from such environments:

- **Actors** represent human players or processes involved in the system;
- **Assets** can be either **items** or **data**;
- **Locations** represent where actors or items may be situated either physically or digitally;
- **Edges** describe possible relocation paths between locations;
- **Policies** describe access control and specify allowed actions, *e.g.*, get some data item from a location or move between locations; and
- **Processes** formalize certain state transition mechanisms, *e.g.*, computer programs or virtual machines.

Unlike in the real world, there is no satellite to provide pictures of the environment. The model creation is instead the result of a collection of processes that resemble the combination of satellite and geographer. Before the actual model creation can start, information about the system needs to be gathered. This happens in several parallel processes, both via a specially crafted user interface and automated data acquisition, *e.g.*, in case of large IT infrastructures.

When using a real map for navigation, the goal is to reach a certain location under certain constraints, *e.g.*, as fast as possible, as economical as possible, or without using freeways. Once a system model is built, the attack navigator needs an *attacker goal* to explore the ways to achieve this goal by moving through the model. The goal itself is stated as a policy violation, *e.g.*, illegitimate access to a data asset, and as such can serve as a trigger for an automated navigation procedure.

At this point, navigation through a system model and orienteering across a terrain start to differ. As mentioned above, finding one's way in nature or urban environment usually has a well-set optimisation goal, typically path length or time that it would take to follow this path.

Navigation through a system model is relatively less understood and the methods of along-the-path optimisation are much less mature than shortest path algorithms on terrain graphs. Hence, the output of an attack navigator, in terms of possible attack scenarios, has to contain more information and optimisation itself has to happen at a later stage.

In case of the current toolset implementation of TRE$_S$PASS, this output contains formal attack vector descriptions in the form of attack trees [5]. This is not the only possible option, but attack trees were chosen since they are rather well established and accepted in the risk assessment community [6]. Also, computational methods have been developed for various optimisation targets that can be stated for attack trees [7–10].

After the analysis of the attack trees has been finished, the results are displayed to the end user on a visual front-end. The user can then take decisions concerning overall security level, required additional controls and possible model updates. After the model has been updated, the analysis can be run again to study the effects of the changes on the security level.

3   The Attack Navigator

We will now look closer at the attack navigator itself. Car navigation systems are independent of the car they are used in, *i.e.*, properties of the car are often ignored since they typically are the same for each car. The navigator may have options to avoid, for example, unpaved roads in non-4WD cars but these options are not explicitly linked to types of cars.

In the attack navigator, the important properties that influence the possible attacks are properties of the attacker. Just as in car navigation systems, in many current models of security risk, these attacker properties are implicit. The risks and identified attacks by such methods are annotated with probability, time, and cost values, which are based on assumptions on the attacker that tries to perform the attack.

Threat agent modelling [11–13] aims at specifying explicit threat agents as a basis for security risk assessment, with properties such as skill, resources, and objectives. This may lead to profiles such as activists, terrorists, or spies all with specific properties.

The TREsPASS attack navigator concept takes an important step beyond current models of security risk by leveraging threat agents as attacker profiles. The attack navigator analysis uses a combination of a navigator map and an attacker profile to derive

- suitable goals for the attacker based on attacker motivation, and
- feasible routes to that goal and properties of these routes based on skill and resources from the attacker profile.

The attacker profiles also imply a link between attack navigators and security economics [14]. Both attackers and defenders have costs for their actions, and utility functions associated with the possible outcomes, but only a limited budget. The utility of attackers may be different based on their motivation, and this can be used in the analysis of attack trees [15]. The attack navigator aims at optimising defender investments, assuming that

- attackers optimise their investments as well,
- the defender moves before the attacker, and
- the attacker knows what the defender has done.

This amounts to a simple two-step game with minimax optimisation [16]. One can also consider attacker behaviour over time in order to get frequency metrics for risk analysis [17].

The similarity with economic models also means that there is quite a bit of uncertainty in the results of computations. The assumptions made may not always hold, and the available data is fragile. The claim of attack navigators is therefore not a precise prediction of what will happen, but rather a prediction of what is possible or likely, and to what extent countermeasures improve the situation. Even if results are not the exact numbers we would like to have, they can be useful for comparing options, or even as thinking tools for imagining possible attacks.

4 From Satellite View to Maps

An essential component of a navigator is the underlying map, on which routes are computed. As such they also form an important component of the attack navigator. Maps of the real world are created based on satellite images and the work by geographers. This approach is only partly feasible for creating maps of organisations: while the overall building structure can be assessed from the outside, elements such as access control policies or network and social structures cannot. These elements, however, form an essential part of attack navigator maps, since they can be enabling factors of attacks, *i.e.*, routes through the navigator map. Satellites are not the right tool for another reason: the organisations under scrutiny are typically rather small and consequently also only cover a limited area. If the attack navigator map covers a bigger area, this part of reality can usually be represented by parts of a real map.

4.1 Models of Reality

When creating maps as models of reality, one needs to abstract the real world by a concept that is suited for automated detection of routes. For real navigation systems, maps are stored as graphs with nodes connected by edges; both nodes and edges can have properties, *e.g.*, size of a city, size of a street, or whether it is open for traffic or not.

Models for attack navigators follow the same approach: organisations are abstracted to graphs, nodes in the graph represent locations in the organisation,

Table 1. An overview of components in the attack navigator map and the tools and processes to identify them.

Real world	Model component	Tool
Relevant area	Locations and edges	Maps
Computer networks	Assets and edges	Network exploration tools such as **nmap** to explore network infrastructure.
Human actors	Actors	Demographic surveys, personnel profiles
Physical access control	Policies and processes	Documents and interviews
Computer access control	Policies and processes	Documents, extraction tools, interviews
Software processes	Processes	Documents, extraction tools, interviews

and edges between nodes represent connectivity between these locations. The construction of attack navigator maps follows a different approach than for real maps, though. As mentioned above, satellites are not really applicable. They can, however, serve as a metaphor. Where satellite pictures give a view of the real world that needs to be interpreted to create a map, tools can be used to obtain a similar view of organisations.

For creating attack navigator maps, a collection of tools or processes are required to collect information about the different parts of an organisation and its surroundings as necessary for the map. Table 1 shows components of attack navigator maps and tools and processes to collect them. In general, whenever adding a new category to be represented in attack navigator maps, one will also need to add a new tool or process to collect the necessary information.

As shown in Table 1, quite a number of components are obtained through interviews or by running tools. This is where the *modeller*, the attack navigator map's equivalent of the geographer, becomes important. Like the geographer is in charge of assembling the map, and interpreting parts of the satellite image, the modeller is in charge of integrating the bits and pieces of infrastructure and data. Especially the interview parts require special attention, since extracting and interpreting the information obtained through interviews is difficult.

In the TRE$_S$PASS project, a set of tools for physical modelling have been developed [18] to structure the interview process; physical modelling enables employees to contribute to the map creation as domain experts with inside knowledge of their organisation and its policies, assets and values. Physical modelling provides a way to engage employees into the map creation, and to give them a creative process to provide input.

The attack navigator map is constructed around the mapping of locations together. The locations in the different infrastructures establish the connection points between the different layers of the organisation. Access control policies are associated with locations in the building layer and assets in the network layer. Locations in the network layer can coincide with locations in the building layer. Assets are located at other assets or at locations of the network or building layer. Attack navigator maps are structured using these co-locations.

Figure 1 shows a small example for a navigator map with different locations, actors, and assets. In the office there is a safe with a secret in it, and Bob has a key to open the safe. There is another key on the shelf in the reception. Alice wants to obtain the secret from the safe, but the safe has a policy that requires actors to have the matching key in order to open the safe and access its content. Accessing content is represented as input in system models.

4.2   Policies

Policies play an important role in attack navigator maps, since they describe how access to certain nodes is restricted, and what an actor in the model needs to fullfil to access the annotated location or asset. Examples include key cards or keys that are required to access a door. Besides these *local* policies, there also exist system-wide or *global* policies [19]. Global policies identify the assets of

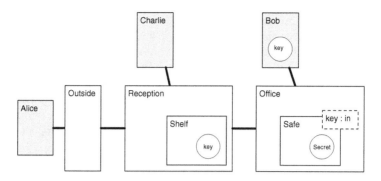

Fig. 1. Example for a small system model with several actors, locations, and assets.

an organisation that should be protected against attackers. For example, they might specify that a certain file type is not allowed to leave the organisation, or that a certain location may only be entered at certain times or with a set of credentials. Section 5 discusses how these global policies guide the computation of attacker routes.

4.3   Model Patterns

Like real maps, attack navigator maps tend to contain components that are similar to each other; they share the same structure, but might be different with respect to some properties. For creating maps, there exist standards of such patterns used by map editors.

For attack navigator maps, patterns are equally important since many elements occur repeatedly. To ease the modeller's task, model patterns are provided in a library. Model patterns are sub-graphs that can be put into the attack navigator map. When such a pattern is put into the map, it is instantiated and can be configured to match the element of the real world it represents.

Model patterns also include policies and processes, which represent access control restrictions and functionality at nodes in the model. For access control or for modelling, *e.g.*, network infrastructure, policies and processes can be combined to model quite complex scenarios. For example, role-based access control can be modelled by allowing different roles to output different messages to a location, where each message triggers a process that implements the assigned functionality.

5   From Maps to Routes

Once an organisation has been represented using a graphical model, the attack navigator can identify possible routes on the map for the attacker to reach a goal [20,21]. In this section we discuss the different steps in doing so. After introducing the representation of attacker routes in the next part, we discuss the actual attack navigation and attack patterns, which can be used to extend identified attack in a similar way as the model patterns discussed in the previous section.

Like real navigation, attack navigation is white-box testing of a map. We assume that the attacker has perfect knowledge of the organisation and knows, *e.g.*, where assets are located, what the layout of the organisation is, or how employees can be social engineered. Scenarios with incomplete knowledge can be considered as well, *i.e.*, an attacker who needs to explore the organisation, but then the impact of attacks can be expected to be lower than for an attacker with perfect knowledge.

5.1   Attacker Routes

Before presenting the actual routing mechanism on attack navigator maps, we briefly discuss the representation of routes. In a navigation system, routes are series of coordinates, often with information about potential congestion on that part of the route. A navigation system assumes that its user is rational and will follow the suggested route. Only once deviations from that route are observed, it will start to recalculate a new route from the position where the user is at this point.

Attacker routes are computed slightly differently, and consequently need another representation. For attacker routes, we are interested in all possible attacks. As described above, the result of the attack navigator is the set of all attacks that are possible in the model, quantified by some property, and ranked accordingly. This is similar to the regular navigator: for navigation, only the shortest, fastest, or most economic route is displayed. Due the complexity of attacks, this selection is far from easy for the attack navigator; the result is therefore presented to a human defender who will dismiss impossible or negligible attacks.

To enable this selection process, attack trees [5,6] are the ideal representation, since they combine different possible attacks that lead to the same goal. The root of an attack tree represents this goal, and the subtrees represent sub-attacks that either need all to be fulfilled, or where one is sufficient to reach the goal. For representing attacker routes, the former would represent that several steps need to be taken, and the latter would represent different possible routes. We present examples for attack trees in Fig. 5.

5.2   Attack Identification

Attack identification is the actual navigation on the attack navigator map. Like real navigation, it takes an attacker location and identifies a possible route from this location to the desired goal.

For the attack navigator map shown in Fig. 1, the goal is clear: Alice wants to obtain the secret from the safe. Once the goal is identified, the paths to the goal (only one in the example) and the missing assets are identified. Alice lacks the key, which is available from Bob or from the Shelf. The upper part of Fig. 5 shows part of the attack tree generated for this scenario.

Goal Identification: As discussed above, the goal in attack navigator maps is identified based on global policies of the modelled organisation. These policies represent a goal of the organisation that should not be violated. Examples include that employees should not send secret files by email, that in general secret files should not leave the organisation, or that the password file on a computer may not be read. In the attacker route, this goal would be the root node, and its children would represent different attacks that enable an attacker to reach this goal.

The result of the goal identification is an action, which the attacker tries to perform, or an asset, which the attacker tries to possess. An important observation is that the latter is a variant of the former; to possess an asset, the attacker needs to perform an action to obtain it. In the attack navigator, this is represented as inputting the asset.

Attack Paths: For each of the identified attacker goals, there may exist numerous paths to reach the goal location, where the goal action can be performed, or where the goal asset can be obtained. The attack navigation considers all these paths, since they may result in different impact or may otherwise have different properties that the defender deems important.

This property is essentially different from standard navigation, where it is a safe assumption that one can ignore routes that are too slow compared to the optimal routes at any given point during routing. Attacker routes are only evaluated in the next step and a defender might use different criteria for evaluating trees; as a result, there is no decision basis for ignoring attack routes or for evaluating them on the fly. One important evaluation criteria is an attack route's impact, which does not increase continuously, but may have discontinuous changes based, *e.g.*, on the assets obtained.

Every step in an attack path consists of a step in the model, be it moving from one location to another, or be it obtaining some asset—either the final one, or one that is needed to perform some other action. For example, if the attacker goal is to read the password file on a central server, then the root password of that machine is an asset that needs to be obtained.

Required Resources: These required resources are acquired on the fly. Whenever the attacker encounters an action in an attack path that requires an asset such as the password for the server machine, a new attack is spawned, at the end of which the attacker has obtained that asset. It is important to note that the routes always assume success, even though an attack might be prohibited. From the attacker's viewpoint the asset has been obtained, and the original attack can continue as planned. This should also be the defender's point of view—the interesting case is not a defeated attack, but a successful one.

Moving Assets: Finally, attacker routes can differ significantly from normal routes through the fact that the goal asset in attacker models can move or be moved, resulting in novel attacks. In a regular navigation system this would mean that the goal could be moved, resulting in a shorter, faster, or longer trip.

While this is not possible for real goals, it is a common attack strategy in attacker maps: The attack consists in making the asset move, and then finding attacks to all those locations that the asset can reach. The means of making an asset move differ depending on the kind of asset. Data usually moves through processes, which are triggered by the attacker; assets usually move with actors, which an attacker must social engineer.

An example for an attack that made the data move is a cloud service administrator who attached a network sniffer to the local network in the server room, and then made a virtual machine migrate from one server to another; as a result, the administrator had a copy of the network traffic that he could playback to obtain a copy of the virtual machine.

5.3   Detailedness of Models

One general issue with maps and routes, both for real maps and attack navigator maps, is the level of detail in the maps. In both cases, if the maps are too detailed, it is very difficult to identify a close-to-optimal route; if the maps however are too imprecise, the routes are not realistic either, and may lack important information needed to follow the route.

In attack navigator maps, the level of detail relates to how detailed the identified attacks are. Coming back to the cloud administrator example, modelling the bits and bytes of the virtual machine and the OSI network stack is likely too much detail. On the other hand, in a system that models only the two servers not including the network infrastructure, it will not be possible to identify the attack at all.

The level of detail is therefore an important design criteria when designing (attack navigator) maps. A good guiding principle is to include only those elements that are essential for the functionality of the overall system, but exclude internal workings of the system. The modelling work in the TRE$_S$PASS project has shown that it is better to exclude some details and to rely on attack patterns to add possible attack steps to the generated attack route.

5.4   Attack Patterns

To deal with detailedness of models, and the resulting detailedness of attacks, we introduce attack patterns, which are similar to the model patterns discussed in the previous section. For too detailed models it is difficult to deal with the resulting overly detailed attack trees. For models with too few details, this is equally difficult. However, it is easier to add "standard" attack pattens to an attack tree, than it is to remove superfluous nodes.

Attack patterns identify typical approaches to performing an attack. Since they are used to extend the attacker routes or attack trees introduced earlier, attack patterns are represented as subtrees as well.

```
 1  label match {
 2    case IN attacker item container:
 3      // get type attacker from attacker profile
 4      // get type item from knowledge base
 5      // get type container from knowledge base
 6      // insert APL attacks that allow to extract item from container
 7    case MAKE attacker actor action:
 8      // get type attacker from attacker profile
 9      // get type actor from attacker profile
10      // insert APL attacks based on types and action
11    //...
12  }
```

Fig. 2. Code for the expansion of general attack trees in a context-unaware fashion. The expansion algorithm iterates over all leaf nodes and matches leaf node labels against the known cases. If a leaf node label matches a pattern in the attack pattern library, it is inserted into the general attack tree. Figure 5 illustrates this process.

Attack patterns are applied by inspecting the actions in an attack tree, and by exploring whether a certain action realisations of this action are known. The overall structure of this exploration is shown in Fig. 2: The expansion algorithm iterates over all leaf nodes and matches the action at this leaf (represented as leaf node labels) against the known cases. If a leaf node label matches a pattern in the attack pattern library, it is inserted into the general attack tree.

This approach has a number of benefits beyond it contributing to clearing out models and keeping them free of clutter. Attack pattern libraries can be shared between organisations to disseminate findings about possible attacks. Once an attack pattern is available in the attack navigator, whenever a matching action working on matching types of assets or actors is found, the pattern will be instantiated.

Two attack patterns are shown in Figs. 3 and 4. The pattern in Fig. 3 replaces obtaining an item from an actor with either stealing the item or social engineering the actor to give it to the attacker. The root of the pattern specifies the action and the types of the arguments for the actor A obtaining an item I from an actor C, represented as A inputing I from C:

$$IN\ A\ item : I\ actor : C$$

This information is crucial for applying the pattern, also because these arguments A (attacker), I (item), and C (actor) occur again in the attack pattern, and must be replaced with the matching values from the attack tree.

The pattern in Fig. 4 is a bit more complicated; it describes that A makes B perform some action for him. As before, the root of the pattern is replaced with nodes that represent different alternatives in the attack. It should be noted that later phases may discard some of the generated attacks since they might be infeasible.

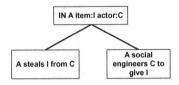

Fig. 3. An attack pattern that replaces the action of obtaining (inputting) an item from an actor with two attacks, one stealing the item from the actor, and the other one social engineering the actor to hand over the item.

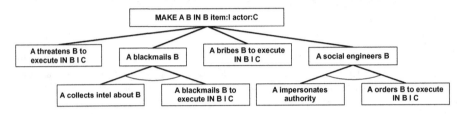

Fig. 4. An attack pattern that replaces social engineering an actor A to obtain (input) an item from another actor B. The alternatives inserted are threatening, blackmailing, bribing, and social engineering actor A to perform the action.

Social Engineering: A typical example for attack steps that should be added through attack patterns, not through adding more details to the model, is social engineering. Social engineering is an important factor of attacking organisations through exploiting the knowledge and the access rights of employees or insiders [22–24]. Social engineering usually requires creating a pretext, which is part of bringing the victim into a situation where it either is not aware of contributing to an attack, or where it has sufficient reason to believe to do the right thing.

Due to its dependency on human behaviour, social engineering is difficult to deal with in formal methods. Since the choice of pretext, for example applying authority, depends heavily on the victim, this kind of attack is best dealt with through attack patterns. The patterns shown in Figs. 3 and 4 introduce social engineering nodes, where the attacker social engineers another actor to perform an action.

5.5   Attacker and Actor Profiles

The success of both attackers and defenders depends on the type of actor and the skills considered. In the attack navigator, different profiles are considered based on threat agent modelling [11–13], which provides skills, resources, and objectives of actors. The attack navigator analysis uses these profiles to identify attacks and countermeasures on a system model, and to predict the likelihood of success and impact of the attack.

Actor profiles separate the planning of a route from its assessment: routes in the attack navigator are *all* possible attacks with respect to the model. Not all of these attacks are feasible for all attackers, but they are still attacks. For car

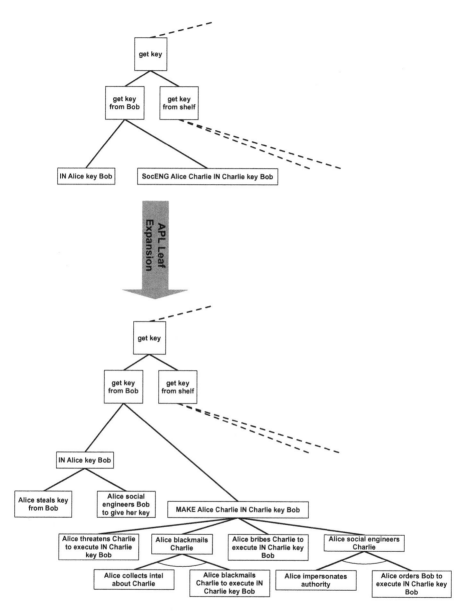

Fig. 5. The expansion of a part of a general attack tree. The patterns (Figs. 3 and 4) may have holes, which are filled with attributes from the leaf node that is expanded. For conjunctive nodes, the outgoing edges are connected with an arc, indicating that all child nodes are required to be executed to reach the goal.

navigation this would mean to show all possible paths from the starting point to the goal, but routes that require a 4WD car would not be feasible for all cars.

Real navigation cannot consider all routes, since it requires the driver to decide, which of the many possible routes is the best with respect to an optimization goal. For attack navigation it is the reverse: a single route or attack out of many is not useful; considering *all* attacks enables the tools to identify countermeasures that disable as many attacks as possible with a certain effort, and it also enables analysis of which kind of attacker to watch out for.

6   Countermeasures

A risk assessment would be useless if it would not come with a way to incorporate countermeasure effect analysis. There are two major ways in which the TRE$_S$PASS methodology supports this.

The first approach is generic and can in principle be applied to any risk assessment framework. It uses the framework as a black box which takes some inputs (in the case of TRE$_S$PASS, the system model) and gives some output (in our case, prioritized attack vectors). Assuming the end user is able to change the model and run the analysis again, we obtain a full operational loop with human involvement, where the user is expected to interpret the analysis results and actively participate in the model development.

Even though TRE$_S$PASS aims at automating the risk analysis process, we do not think that full automation is possible or even needed. Again coming back to the terrain navigation analogue – the human is not expected to follow GPS blindly. In fact, several cases have been reported when people being overconfident in the GPS reading have ended up in serious accidents [25,26]. And even if the model, *i.e.*, the map, used by the GPS device is correct, the user may still have optimization preferences the device is unaware of.

In some sense, the situation is even better with the attack navigator. Here the user has more options than just selecting between the routes offered by a machine. The user can actually change the map by implementing additional controls, increasing efficiency of the existing ones, etc. All these changes would hopefully change the risk landscape, and running the analysis tool again on an updated map is the prime way of verifying this.

As mentioned in Sect. 2, attack trees are not the only possible attack description language that can be used in TRE$_S$PASS. Attack-defence trees by Kordy *et al.* [27] are an alternative approach to countermeasure selection. In principle, this formalism allows for integrating countermeasures into the risk assessment process on a lower level than the generic model update approach described above. It is possible already at the attack generation stage to also generate certain defence nodes into the tree or to obtain those from standard libraries. The option of changing the model and running the analysis again of course remains, so the attack-defence tree approach is potentially more flexible than the one based on classical attack trees. However, since attack-defence trees are considerably more recent and accordingly less studied, the current version of the TRE$_S$PASS toolset (as of 2015) does not yet support this.

7   Conclusions

The navigation metaphor is a new approach to security assessment of complex systems that aims at being more accessible to a human end user than other computer-assisted frameworks. However, no metaphor can make the inherent challenges of risk assessment to go away, it can only try to present them on the level where human decisions can be made more intuitively.

The TRE$_S$PASS project has been building a toolset supporting such a workflow. We have published key innovations in for example the attack navigation metaphor [14], making attacker profiles explicit [28], attack generation [20,21], quantitative analysis [29,30], and visualisation of maps and paths [31,32]. Our practical and theoretical developments open up for many new and interesting research questions in the area of attack navigation and graphical models for security, for example:

- What is the correct abstraction level for a system models and maps that would be humanly comprehensible and at the same time would allow formal analysis?
- Are there additional opportunities for using the properties of attacker profiles in security analysis? Can we use more advanced calculations or statistics?
- Are the current TRE$_S$PASS model components generalisable enough to perform realistic security assessments on a wide class of systems, or are extensions needed for different types of systems?
- How can we share attack patterns and what are the requirements on the pattern sharing authorisation infrastructure?

Acknowledgment. The research leading to these results has received funding from the European Union Seventh Framework Programme (FP7/2007–2013) under grant agreement no. 318003 (TRE$_S$PASS). This publication reflects only the authors' views and the Union is not liable for any use that may be made of the information contained herein.

References

1. Fischhoff, B.: Risk perception and communication unplugged: twenty years of process. Risk Anal. **15**(2), 137–145 (1995)
2. Jasanoff, S.: The political science of risk perception. Reliab. Eng. Syst. Saf. **59**(1), 91–99 (1998)
3. Weinstein, N.D.: What does it mean to understand a risk? evaluating risk comprehension. J. Nat. Cancer Inst. Monogr. **25**, 15–20 (1999)
4. The Consortium: Project webpage, 31 October 2015. https://www.trespass-project.eu
5. Schneier, B.: Attack trees: modeling security threats. Dr. Dobb's J. Softw. Tools **24**(12), 21–29 (1999). http://www.ddj.com/security/184414879
6. Kordy, B., Piètre-Cambacédès, L., Schweitzer, P.: DAG-based attack and defense modeling: don't miss the forest for the attack trees. Comput. Sci. Rev. **13–14**, 1–38 (2014)

7. Jürgenson, A., Willemson, J.: Computing exact outcomes of multi-parameter attack trees. In: Meersman, R., Tari, Z. (eds.) OTM 2008, Part II. LNCS, vol. 5332, pp. 1036–1051. Springer, Heidelberg (2008)

8. Jürgenson, A., Willemson, J.: Serial model for attack tree computations. In: Lee, D., Hong, S. (eds.) ICISC 2009. LNCS, vol. 5984, pp. 118–128. Springer, Heidelberg (2010)

9. Jürgenson, A., Willemson, J.: On fast and approximate attack tree computations. In: Kwak, J., Deng, R.H., Won, Y., Wang, G. (eds.) ISPEC 2010. LNCS, vol. 6047, pp. 56–66. Springer, Heidelberg (2010)

10. Arnold, F., Hermanns, H., Pulungan, R., Stoelinga, M.: Time-dependent analysis of attacks. In: Abadi, M., Kremer, S. (eds.) POST 2014 (ETAPS 2014). LNCS, vol. 8414, pp. 285–305. Springer, Heidelberg (2014)

11. Casey, T.: Threat Agent Library Helps Identify Information Security Risks. Intel White Paper, Houston (2007)

12. Casey, T., Koeberl, P., Vishik, C.: Threat agents: a necessary component of threat analysis. In: Proceedings of the Sixth Annual Workshop on Cyber Security and Information Intelligence Research, CSIIRW 2010, pp. 56:1–56:4. ACM, New York (2010)

13. Rosenquist, M.: Prioritizing Information Security Risks with Threat Agent Risk Assessment. Intel White Paper, Houston (2010)

14. Pieters, W., Barendse, J., Ford, M., Heath, C.P., Probst, C.W.: The navigation metaphor in security economics. IEEE Secur. Priv. **14**, Scheduled for publication in May/June 2016

15. Van Holsteijn, R.: The motivation of attackers in attack tree analysis. Master's thesis, TU Delft (2015)

16. Cox Jr, L.A.: Game theory and risk analysis. Risk Anal. **29**(8), 1062–1068 (2009)

17. Pieters, W., Davarynejad, M.: Calculating adversarial risk from attack trees: control strength and probabilistic attackers. In: Garcia-Alfaro, J., Herrera-Joancomartí, J., Lupu, E., Posegga, J., Aldini, A., Martinelli, F., Suri, N. (eds.) DPM/SETOP/QASA 2014. LNCS, vol. 8872, pp. 201–215. Springer, Heidelberg (2015)

18. The Consortium: Final requirements for visualisation processes and tools Deliverable D4.1.2 (2015)

19. Pieters, W., Dimkov, T., Pavlovic, D.: Security policy alignment: a formal approach. IEEE Syst. J. **7**(2), 275–287 (2013)

20. Kammüller, F., Probst, C.W.: Invalidating policies using structural information. In: 2nd International IEEE Workshop on Research on Insider Threats (WRIT 2013). IEEE Co-located with IEEE CS Security and Privacy 2013 (2013)

21. Kammüller, F., Probst, C.W.: Combining generated data models with formal invalidation for insider threat analysis. In: 3rd International IEEE Workshop on Research on Insider Threats (WRIT 2014). IEEE Co-located with IEEE CS Security and Privacy 2014 (2014)

22. Winkler, I.S., Dealy, B.: Information security technology? don't rely on it. a case study in social engineering. In: USENIX Security (1995)

23. Thornburgh, T.: Social engineering: the "dark art". In: Proceedings of the 1st Annual Conference on Information Security Curriculum Development, InfoSecCD 2004, pp. 133–135. ACM, New York (2004)

24. Mitnick, K.D., Simon, W.L., Wozniak, S.: The Art of Deception: Controlling the Human Element of Security. Wiley, Hoboken (2002)

25. Holley, P.: Driver follows GPS off demolished bridge, killing wife, police say, 15 October 2015. https://www.washingtonpost.com/news/morning-mix/wp/2015/03/31/driver

26. Knudson, T.: 'Death by GPS' in desert, Last visited 15 October 2015 (2011). http://www.sacbee.com/entertainment/living/travel/article2573180.html

27. Kordy, B., Mauw, S., Radomirović, S., Schweitzer, P.: Attack-defense trees. J. Log. Comput. **24**(1), 55–87 (2014)

28. Lenin, A., Willemson, J., Sari, D.P.: Attacker profiling in quantitative security assessment based on attack trees. In: Bernsmed, K., Fischer-Hübner, S. (eds.) NordSec 2014. LNCS, vol. 8788, pp. 199–212. Springer, Heidelberg (2014)

29. Buldas, A., Lenin, A.: New efficient utility upper bounds for the fully adaptive model of attack trees. In: Das, S.K., Nita-Rotaru, C., Kantarcioglu, M. (eds.) GameSec 2013. LNCS, vol. 8252, pp. 192–205. Springer, Heidelberg (2013)

30. Lenin, A., Willemson, J., Charnamord, A.: Genetic approximations for the failure-free security games. In: Khouzani, M.H.R., et al. (eds.) GameSec 2015. LNCS, vol. 9406, pp. 311–321. Springer, Heidelberg (2015). doi:10.1007/978-3-319-25594-1_17

31. Hall, P., Heath, C., Coles-Kemp, L., Tanner, A.: Examining the contribution of critical visualisation to information security. In: Proceedings of the 2015 New Security Paradigms Workshop. ACM (2015)

32. Heath, C.H.P., Coles-Kemp, L., Hall, P.A., et al.: Logical lego? co-constructed perspectives on service design. In: DS 81: Proceedings of NordDesign 2014, Espoo, Finland, 27–29th August 2014

Integrated Visualization of Network Security Metadata from Heterogeneous Data Sources

Volker Ahlers(✉), Felix Heine, Bastian Hellmann, Carsten Kleiner, Leonard Renners, Thomas Rossow, and Ralf Steuerwald

Faculty IV, Department of Computer Science, University of Applied Sciences and Arts Hannover, P.O. Box 920251, 30441 Hannover, Germany
volker.ahlers@hs-hannover.de, trust@f4-i.fh-hannover.de
http://trust.f4.hs-hannover.de/

Abstract. In computer networks many components produce valuable information about themselves or other participants, especially security analysis relevant information. Although such information is intrinsically related as components are connected by a network, most of them still operate independently and do not share data amongst each other. Furthermore, the highly dynamic nature of a network hampers a profound understanding of security relevant situations, such as attack scenarios. Hence, a comprehensive view of the network including multiple information sources as well as temporal network evolution would significantly improve security analysis and evaluation capabilities. In this paper, we introduce a comprehensive approach for an integrated visualization, covering all aspects from data acquisition in various sources up to visual representation of the integrated information. We analyze the requirements on the basis of an exemplary scenario, propose solutions covering these demands based on the IF-MAP protocol, and introduce our software application VisITMeta as a prototypical implementation. We show how the graph-based IF-MAP protocol provides a graphical model for an integrated view of network security.

1 Introduction

In recent years several visualization approaches have been proposed for network security components like Intrusion Detection System (IDS and flow controllers, which monitor different aspects of network traffic or the behavior of systems and users [11]. For a comprehensive view on the overall network state, however, an integrated visualization of security information gathered from multiple separate components is desirable. In contrast to existing dashboard user interfaces, which visualize information from different sources in separate views on the same screen, we aim at the visualization of homogenized data within a single representation to emphasize their interrelations. In this way, the user can get a thorough understanding of well-defined aspects of the network by focusing on its immediate surroundings, while still being able to gain a broad overview of the network by including more generally related data, e.g. infrastructure information. An integrated visualization thereby facilitates a detailed assessment of the security state and the detection of potential security threats or attacks.

© Springer International Publishing Switzerland 2016
S. Mauw et al. (Eds.): GraMSec 2015, LNCS 9390, pp. 18–34, 2016.
DOI: 10.1007/978-3-319-29968-6_2

1.1   Exemplary Real World Scenario

The following scenario clarifies the necessity of those advanced monitoring and visualization approaches and serves as a basis for the requirements we derive for our approach. Given is a typical enterprise environment with several employees, each with a personal computer or smartphone. They are part of a network, which includes services, like mail and SSH servers, internal storage devices, and databases. An IDS is used to detect unwanted behavior and firewalls regulate the traffic and enforce the security policy.

One possible attack scenario is a user downloading an infected file (not recognized by the IDS), which results in compromising his account and device. The malware not only starts to spread across the internal network, but also tries to compromise further accounts by conducting brute-force login attempts onto available services within the network (this finally is detected by the IDS). Subsequently systems successfully infected start doing the same.

The desired process for a network security administrator is to: (1) Quickly detect not only single incidents, but recognize the combination of failed login attempts on multiple services by the same users. (2) Find the sources of the attacks and thereby the infected systems and users (they might use different login information or spoofed addresses). (3) Discover the initial security breach by identifying the initially infected component and determine the way the malware entered the network. (4) React as fast as possible (e.g., shut down accounts or lock out devices) to prevent further harm, like successful brute-force attempts. (5) Return the network as well as its components and users towards a productive state after the problem has been handled appropriately.

1.2   Requirements

A tool which helps the security administrator perform tasks as in Sect. 1.1 has to fulfill three main requirements, each of which with suitable visual support.

(I) *Real-time Monitoring.* Due to the highly dynamic nature of networks, time is a crucial factor when analyzing the network state. Fast reactions can prevent other systems from getting corrupted or valuable information from getting stolen. Furthermore, analysis results may only be accurate for a certain time frame, and it is crucial to acquire knowledge before it is outdated.

(II) *Data Integration.* The different network components generally perform their respective tasks without communicating with each other or sharing their available information, most of them using proprietary data models. To overcome these isolated views, an integration of the different parts of information is fundamental. Nevertheless, the source of each datum should still be retained, in order to correlate achieved knowledge on a semantically higher level with the triggering low level events.

(III) *Retrospective Analysis.* In order to understand the current state of a network it is necessary not only to perceive and detect current situations, but to retrace the events which have led to the current state. Hence, tracking the changes within the network is unavoidable and certain access mechanisms offer different advantages in the analysis. A playback of the events between two states enables an easier understanding of the transition from a desired towards an undesired state of a device or network, whereas replication of a single previous state can be used to review and restore an older configuration.

1.3   Contribution and Outline

In this paper we show how the Interface for Metadata Access Points (IF-MAP), a graph-based framework to manage metadata from multiple data sources in an integrated fashion, can be used as a foundation to collect information from different services, infrastructure components and endpoints for integrated visualization. While graphs provide natural representations of network topologies, IF-MAP also uses graphs to model relations between logical network components, like device addresses or user identities, and accompanying metadata, like capabilities, authentication information, or security-related events. Accordingly, the visualization of MAP graphs described in this paper allows a deeper view on the network state and enables correlation of security-relevant information on different semantic levels.

The remainder of this paper is organized as follows. Section 2 provides an overview of related work on the visualization of security information from multiple data sources. In Sects. 3 to 5 solution approaches for the requirements stated above are developed. Section 6 introduces the VisITMeta application, which implements the proposed solutions. Section 7 shows the benefits of the proposed systems and the challenges that were recognized. Section 8 gives a conclusion and an overview of future work.

2   Related Work

OSSIM[1] (Open Source Security Information Management, commercial version: USM) is an open-source Security information and event management (SIEM) system which integrates a collection of other well known open source security systems (e.g., OSSEC, OpenVAS, Snort and Nagios) into one unified system. OSSIM collects information from these systems in a central place for analysis purposes. The analysis results and the raw data are available for oversight by human security experts via a web interface. In addition OSSIM employs pattern and anomaly detection techniques as well as a general model for event correlation, which operates based on event streams or using heuristic algorithms [7].

VIAssist[2] is a commercial visual analysis platform which collects network flow and security data from different sources (e.g., Netflow, IDS) and uses a

---

[1] http://www.alienvault.com/open-threat-exchange/projects.
[2] http://securedecisions.com/products/viassist/.

dashboard with various visualization options [6]. The approach of VIAssist is to offer parallel views of the same or related data in order to facilitate threat detection by visual correlation. In contrast to our approach, both OSSIM and VIAssist use dashboards to visualize security information of different sources and analysis results, but no integrated graphical model. We consider such a model to be extremely important to gain deeper insight into more complex security threats.

Prelude OSS[3] (commercial version: Prelude Pro) is an open-source SIEM system. Prelude collects security-related information from various sources like network sensors, network infrastructure, service end-points and other security systems. Prelude is able to read alarm information in different formats (e.g. flat log files or syslog) and normalize this information to the Intrusion Detection Message Exchange Format (IDMEF) [5]. This normalized information is then stored in a central database and available for third-party software or via the Prelude web interface called *Prewikka*. Prelude includes a rule-based correlation engine called *Prelude-Correlator* which is able to detect security incidents and raise new IDMEF alerts [14]. In contrast to our approach Prelude has a focus on alert information, whereas we suggest to collect all relevant information, which includes alarm information but extends the set of relevant information to infrastructure data (e.g., location and configuration of devices) as well as high-level information like user login patterns.

In [10] a graph-based visualization of data stored in a SIEM system is described. While attack graphs are also used to visualize security incidents, the prototype in the paper neither uses an extensible graph model such as IF-MAP as foundation to store relevant data. Also, it does not provide the historical and progression views of the metadata graph as our approach does.

In summary, the described systems use dashboard-style visualizations of security data from different network components, while we propose an integrated, graph-based visualization. Furthermore we focus on the visualization of network history and temporal development, which none of these systems allows.

TVi [4] and ENAVis [8,9] are approaches to visualize network dynamics with regard to network security. TVi displays time lines of entropies of certain network features. ENAVis is a visual analytics tool that constructs different graphs from network data (e.g., host-host, user-user, host-user, or user-application interactions) and visualizes them using different layouts (force-directed, bipartite). ENAVis allows to find clusters and study similarities between network states at different times by means of visual analysis. While TVi visualizes the temporal evolution of network statistics (entropies, histograms), ENAVis uses an approach similar to ours by modeling different relations within a network as graphs (not restricted to device connections or packet flow) and allowing to review network changes by graph comparison. Our approach goes one step further by integrating different types of relations into a single graph, using metadata to differentiate between relation types. For the visualization of network history we use a

---

[3] https://www.prelude-ids.org/.

different approach based on graph deltas, i.e., sets of newly created and deleted nodes and edges within a selectable time interval.

In [1] we proposed a mechanism for the persistence of MAP data and the computation of graph deltas. A brief overview is given in Sect. 4 below. In the present paper we put this persistence mechanism in a wider context and focus on the integration of multiple data sources as well as visualization of MAP graphs.

3   Integration of Data Sources

As explained in the introduction, only the integration of multiple information sources—such as security-critical events, device configurations, and network topology—can provide a comprehensive view of the overall network state. In order to achieve a common knowledge base, a homogenization of these data sources is required.

Obviously, physical and logical network topology are of great interest for security analysis. Furthermore, configuration, state, and behavioral data of each participant in the network are essential to make a statement about the role of the devices and whether they behave in a desired manner. The collection of this information is not necessarily limited to end-user devices, like desktop computers or smartphones, but includes infrastructural components such as Network Access Control (NAC) systems, switches, or routers. A major challenge is posed by the heterogeneous and distributed nature of the data and its producers. Hence, it is important to combine all data into a common representation by performing homogenization as early as possible.

We suggest using IF-MAP as a protocol since it matches the given requirements for data integration (compare Sect. 1.2) by offering a standardized and extensible data model and a centralized communication model, which conserves the publisher of each information. By using a standardized data model, an implicit homogenization of data is already given and the process of homogenization is sourced out to a data-gathering client. Furthermore several of those clients for data acquisition already exist. In the following, we will provide a basic introduction to IF-MAP and describe its application in our architecture.

3.1   IF-MAP

IF-MAP is an open standard published as part of the Trusted Network Connect (TNC) framework by the Trusted Computing Group (TCG). It defines an XML-based client-server protocol for the exchange of *metadata* between many Metadata Access Point (MAP) clients and a central MAP server. The main specification defines a core data model with basic operations MAP clients and MAP servers have to support and their encapsulation within SOAP [12]. Metadata in IF-MAP are defined in an extensible way, offering the possibility to use IF-MAP for arbitrary domains. Additional specifications describe metadata for, e.g., the domains of network security or security in industrial control systems.

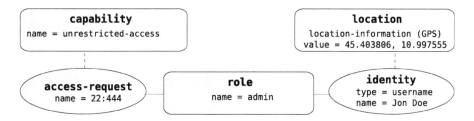

Fig. 1. Example MAP graph: ellipses represent identifiers, rectangles represent metadata, both of which are modeled as different types of nodes. Edges represent relations between identifiers and metadata. In this representation, links are implicitly shown via their attributed metadata connecting two identifier nodes, such as *role*.

IF-MAP Data Model. The data model of IF-MAP consists of an undirected graph that allows cycles and loops. There are three basic data types in IF-MAP: (1) Entities in the domain are described as *identifiers* represented by nodes in the graph, (2) Relations between these entities are called *links* and are represented by edges, (3) Any additional information for an entity or a relation is described as *metadata* and can be attached to both identifiers or links. Identifiers and metadata have a *type* definition, such as identity or location. Furthermore they potentially have different *attributes* like name or value. Metadata additionally have a mandatory *cardinality*, which expresses whether one type of metadata can be attached exactly once (singleValue) or multiple times (multiValue) to the same identifier or link. Figure 1 depicts a simplified example graph using some of the standard elements for network security [13]. Management information like the cardinality, timestamp, or publisher-id are omitted for reasons of clarity.

IF-MAP Communication Model. The communication model of IF-MAP is a content-based publish-subscribe model. Both publishers and subscribers are MAP clients that exchange information with a MAP server. To attach data to the graph structure in the MAP server, clients use the *publish update* operation providing either an identifier and the metadata that is to be attached to it or two identifiers and the metadata to be attached to the link between them. Clients can also delete data from the graph using the *publish delete* operation and similar parameters. Additionally, metadata can be propagated using the *notify* mechanism. Metadata propagated by this mechanism are not attached permanently to the graph structure but only forwarded to the clients holding a subscription that matches the identifier involved. Subscriptions themselves are carried out in an asynchronous fashion using a poll and notification scheme.

3.2 System Architecture

Figure 2 depicts the system architecture of our proposal for an IF-MAP based data integration and visualization. At the bottom, several examples for MAP clients are given: The Interconnected-asset Ontology (IO) framework provides

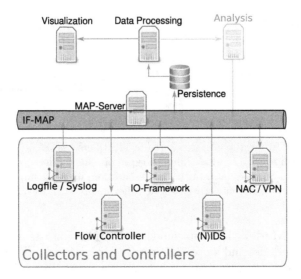

Fig. 2. System architecture overview - arrows depict the data flow

methods to extract the current state of an IT infrastructure [3]. A modified syslog server transforms syslog messages to corresponding IF-MAP metadata, e.g., failed login attempts at an SSH server. Network access mechanisms can publish their knowledge about connecting users and accordingly assigned addresses and accounts. An IDS monitors the network state and communicates incident reporting using IF-MAP. Finally, this information can be used by a flow controller or the network access components to react on specific situations, for example by shutting down a compromised user or device. After the first homogenization, which is implicitly performed by the clients when generating IF-MAP data, the information are gathered at the central MAP server. The MAP server only preserves the current state of the network, while historical information or temporal progress are not recorded. Therefore, a persistence component is needed to gain insight in progression of network state. An analysis component like an anomaly detection engine as in [2] can use the historical information to make policy-based decisions if an network threatening event exists and can propagate this by publishing new metadata. A visualization component renders the IF-MAP graphs to enable a better understanding of the network states.

3.3   Application Level Data Model

With the application of IF-MAP a first homogenization is implemented and a first mutual data model is given. Nevertheless, requirement III in Sect. 1.2 shows that the progression of the graph over time has to be taken into account for an appropriate data analysis. Since IF-MAP is designed to only cover the current situation and no historical information, we utilize a slightly varying application level data model to enable a persistent storage and restoration of past graphs' states. A simplified Unified Modeling Language (UML) representation of this data model is depicted in Fig. 3. The IF-MAP data types (`Link`, `Identifier`, `Metadata`) are merely extended with a method yielding a boolean value whether the datum is valid with regard to a particular timestamp (`isValidAt()`). Another deviation from the IF-MAP model is the introduction of a dedicated data structure for the representation of a pair of identifiers (`IdentifierPair`) for implementation reasons.

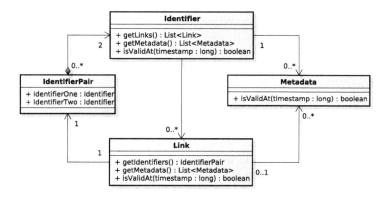

Fig. 3. Application level data model.

4 Persistence Layer Requirements

The requirements for a retrospective analysis also lead to certain consequences for the persistence layer. For example, in order to support *playback* of events, the persistence layer has to provide a query method which yields the graph history step-by-step. In addition, a query mechanism which returns complete snapshots of the graph at any given time is needed for the *replication* part.

In short, the following specific requirements for the graph persistence layer can be directly derived from the need for different forms of retrospective analysis:

(1) *Continuous Recording.* All information related to changes in the graph must be preserved. A snapshot approach which only saves the graph state at constant points in time (and thus aggregates different changes) is not desired.

(2) *State Queries.* It must be possible to query snapshots of a graph at any given time in the history of the graph. The result of such a query must contain the complete graph at that time.

(3) *Change Queries.* It must be possible to query the differences of the graph between two arbitrary points in the graph history.

(4) *Scalability.* Because of the high frequency of changes in a modern network it is necessary that the persistence layer can handle massive amounts of read and write operations. Therefore a solution which can be distributed over multiple hosts and easily scales horizontally is desirable.

To satisfy these demands, we implemented the data acquisition for the persistence as a subscriber to the MAP server, which thereby gets updated on demand and not in fixed intervals. Furthermore we developed algorithms to reconstruct a graph at a given time and to calculate changes between graphs. We chose to model the changes that the graph underwent as an explicit part of the query result. This relieves clients from calculating the actual change between two graph snapshots and directly supports the implementation of such features as "change highlighting". Moreover, this abstract interface can be used as a foundation for the step-by-step query method and can also be used as a building block for other kinds of change-related query or visualization features. For a detailed description of the construction of a graph valid at a given time and how we define and calculate the changes between two points in time (*graph deltas*) see [1].

5   Visualization Concepts

This section introduces the concepts to visualize homogenized data from multiple sources, based on the model described in the previous sections and the requirements stated in Sect. 1.2. Visualizing homogenized and historical information gathered from different data sources allows users to gain insight into the network state and the relationships of logical and physical components. Thus some requirements on the visualization itself have to be fulfilled.

(1) *Representing the Data Model.* The data model as described in different degrees of abstraction in the previous sections forms a graph model with nodes, edges, and metadata attached to both nodes and edges. A visualization of a concrete occurrence of such data must include the entities and their relationships in a distinguishable manner, so that a user can easily separate between them.

(2) *Publisher Distinction.* The possibility to trace the origin of the data is important for the user. As the data itself is homogenized by transmitting it via IF-MAP and arbitrary MAP clients can publish data of the same type, the source of data can only be determined by using the information about the original data source, i.e. the publisher-id of the corresponding MAP client. This information can be used to alter the appearance of the visualized data. It allows to focus on data from a single data source, or to inspect how data from different sources creates a more detailed overview when combined in a single graph, showing relationships that are invisible if the original data is viewed independently.

(3) *History Navigation.* The architecture to persist the history of gathered data and the possibility to retrieve the current state at a given timestamp as well as querying graph deltas between two timestamps requires a proper functionality to navigate in time and to select the mode of data retrieval.

(4) *Clustering of Data.* The integration of formerly independent data sources most likely shows unknown dependencies and relationships between the data. To emphasize them to the user, data should be grouped and arranged in a way that utilizes the semantics of the data, e.g., subgraphs that represent all information about one specific endpoint.

5.1 Graph Visualization

By matching the data model itself general mechanisms to visualize graphs can be used. Identifiers and metadata can be rendered as arbitrary shapes whereas the relationships between identifiers can be rendered as straight lines or curves. The layout of the overall graph and its subgraphs should allow an easy understanding of connections and give a quick glance of the global network state.

5.2 Configurable Color Schemes

One possible way to distinguish data gathered by different data sources in the visualization is to use the information about the publisher of the data itself. By assigning a color value to each publisher—automatically or user defined—the origin of data can be easily determined by the user. Figure 4 shows an MAP graph with colorization according to the publisher ID of the metadata.

In some cases this will lead to equally colored clusters of data, representing data of a single data source that possibly describes a very specific type of information about the network. The total number of different colors shows the amount of data sources involved and therefore visualizes the significance of the data base itself, where fewer data sources could mean a less reliable overview.

All possible IF-MAP identifiers exist at all times, but are seen as valid only when metadata—published by a MAP client—are attached to them. Thus for visualization purposes they can either be colored identically (to distinguish them by color from metadata) or according to their types (e. g. ip-address, mac-address).

5.3 History Navigation

To navigate data in time, the user can switch between three tabs within the graphical user interface: the first one called *live view* always shows the current state of the graph, as stored in the persistence layer. The second tab, *history view*, allows the user to select one of all recorded timestamps including the newest one. A third tab called *delta view* (as shown in Fig. 4) can be used to display the differences in the graph data between two timestamps, as depicted in Sect. 4. Here the user can select both the start and end timestamp for the delta calculation. The graph delta for these two timestamps is retrieved and visualized, with updates and deletes colored or highlighted differently.

Furthermore, the selected interval between start and end timestamp can be moved forward and backward. This is especially useful when selecting a start and end timestamp with an interval of exactly one timestamp, thus showing the changes between two consecutive timestamps; when moving this interval, the user can easily recognize the changes in the graph over time.

The mechanisms to select single timestamps can be implemented in various ways. The simplest way can be a single set of buttons to move forward or backward in time, jumping from one recorded timestamp to the next (or previous).

A timeline with a movable knob can be used to let the user move quickly along time and visualize the instant to which he navigates.

To enhance the selection, the user can be allowed to select a coarse time interval by using input fields or drop-down lists, showing only timestamps at which changes occurred within the persisted data, and then using the timeline to navigate only in the timestamps of that chosen interval. This reduces the amount of snap-in points on the timeline and therefore facilitates navigation.

5.4 Search Functionality and Filtering

To further reduce the amount of data and to only visualize the data relevant to the user, a search functionality as well as filtering is needed. This allows the user to pinpoint a single node, i.e. an identifier or a metadatum, or a selection of nodes with similar features.

The results of the search can be shown by simply highlighting or coloring the matching nodes in a different way than all non-matching nodes. When rendering all non-matching nodes in a lucent way, the user can both easily detect the matching nodes as well as retain the overall graph structure in view.

6 VisITMeta Application

This section introduces the open-source software application VisITMeta (*Visualizing the Security of Modern IT Environments Using Metadata*),[4] which is developed within a research project of the same name with the aim of implementing the concepts described in the previous sections.

6.1 Architecture

The software consists of two different applications. A component called *dataservice* is working as a MAP client and is thus responsible for retrieving information from the MAP server. The data is then persisted in a Neo4j database, using the internal Neo4j data model adjusted to the requirements of storing historical IF-MAP graph data. A REST-like web service interface allows to query the *dataservice* application for the graph at different timestamps, including the current state as well as a list of all timestamps that include changes (updates and deletes), and for graph deltas between two timestamps. The *dataservice* application resembles both the persistence and data processing components of the architecture shown in Fig. 2. The second component called *visualization* uses this interface to fetch graph data and visualizes it by employing the concepts of Sect. 5. It features a graphical user interface that enables the user to navigate through a MAP graph and its history.

---

[4] https://github.com/trustathsh/visitmeta.

6.2   Implemented Features

The VisITMeta application provides the following features to the user:

(1) *General Visualization and Navigation.* The graph layout is performed by the JUNG2 library[5], except for the bipartite layout. In Sect. 6.4 we show some specifics of IF-MAP graph layouting as well as details about the bipartite layout. The results are then rendered via Piccolo2D[6].

(2) *Color-coded Publisher Distinction.* The user can select colors for the originating IF-MAP publishers, which are then used to colorize the shapes used for rendering metadata nodes.

(3) *History Navigation.* Navigation in time is realized via multiple tabs as described in Sect. 5.3; it supports a live view that resembles the current state of the MAP server, as well as views on the history at a given time and graph deltas between two timestamps.

(4) *Highlighting Changes.* When changes in the data occur, updates and deletes are highlighted with colored halos to be recognizable by the user.

(5) *Search Functionality and Filtering.* Search functionality is given by using a textfield and a simple search language, combined with the ability to render non-matching elements in a lucent way.

(6) *Detailed Node Information.* The information of each identifier or metadata node is shown in a separated view on the bottom of the main graph screen. All attributes and elements of the XML data structure underneath each node can be seen, and in case of so called *extended identifier*, a mechanism of IF-MAP to define new identifier types, even the inner information can be seen in a structured way.

(7) *Motion Control.* The visualization application supports external control devices, e.g., the LeapMotion gesture controller.[7]

6.3   Example Illustration

Figure 4 shows the VisITMeta application providing a delta view of an excerpt of the earlier introduced example scenario introduced in Sect. 1.1. In the selected time interval, an external analysis component detected the (not shown) failed login attempts and created an event metadatum indicating a brute force attack. The PDP therefore enforces the disconnection of the aforementioned user, which results in the enforcement-report metadatum.

The green and red halos mark nodes that have been created and deleted, respectively, within the selected time interval, thus showing the creation of the event and enforcement-report and deletion of the subgraph representing the device information and user credentials of the now disconnected endpoint.

The user sees the information gathered by the three components (analysis component, PDP and DHCP server) and how they are related to each other.

---

[5] http://jung.sourceforge.net/.
[6] https://code.google.com/p/piccolo2d/.
[7] https://www.leapmotion.com/.

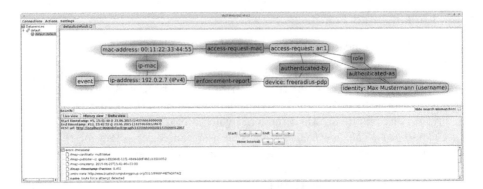

Fig. 4. VisITMeta application showing the example MAP graph with force-directed layout, MAP server connection tree (left), delta navigation (center), and metadata details (bottom). Identifier nodes are depicted by gray rounded rectangles, metadata nodes by rectangles with color coding for publisher distinction (blue: DHCP, violet: PDP, yellow: analysis component) (Color figure online).

Therefore—in this excerpt—the process of detecting malicious behaviour, reacting to it and the result of the reaction can be seen.

The other information are omitted for visibility reasons. VisITMeta could further be used to navigate through the history and track down the user which first started brute forcing (since multiple users might have been affected due to the malware spreading).

The IF-MAP data has been created by the irondemo test suite.[8]

6.4   Specifics of IF-MAP Graph Layouting

A MAP graph in the representation of Fig. 1 consists of two different types of nodes, i.e. nodes for identifiers and metadata. Furthermore, identifier nodes are only connected to metadata nodes, and vice versa. This distinction between graph nodes can be utilized when calculating layouts for the graphical representation of MAP graphs in such a way, that the layout can emphasize their different meaning in a MAP graph. Common layout algorithms could be adjusted to create good distributions of identifier nodes, while clearly positioning metadata nodes belonging to an identifier node near it.

Bipartite Layout. The two distinct types of nodes for identifiers and metadata can be considered as a bipartite graph. VisITMeta makes use of this property by offering a structured—and potentially clearer—graph layout, hereafter named *bipartite layout*. Regarding the specific nature of MAP graphs, i.e., having metadata nodes either connecting two identifier nodes via links or being attributed to single identifier nodes, a variation of the classical two-column (or two-row) layout for bipartite graphs is applied.

---

[8] https://github.com/trustathsh/irondemo.

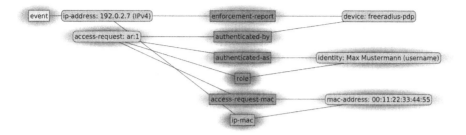

Fig. 5. Bipartite layout applied to the MAP graph of Fig. 4.

It consists of five columns, numbered 1 to 5 for the following explanation. Columns 2 and 4 are designated for identifier nodes. Column 3 is designated for metadata nodes attached to links, thus connecting two identifier nodes.

Columns 1 and 5 are designated for metadata nodes attached to single identifiers that are drawn in column 2 and 4, respectively. Starting from the first identifier node of the current MAP graph, the graph is traversed in depth-first order. Identifier and metadata nodes are drawn from top to bottom in their respective columns, switching from column 2 to 4 (and vice versa) with each metadata node attached to a link (i.e., connecting two identifier nodes).

The example MAP graph from 6.3 with bipartite layout instead of a force-directed layout is shown in Fig. 5. In this case the bipartite layout can be used to recognize the update and delete operations more easily, as they only affect metadata in IF-MAP and the bipartite layout shows them in distinct columns.

7   Discussion of Results

In this section we show some of the benefits our proposed concept of an integrated visualization with a continuous recording might bring the user. We also present some of the challenges we identified during implementing our concept or by findings of using the prototype itself.

7.1   Benefits of an Integrated Visualization with Continuous Recording

(1) *Homogenization.* The graph-based data model of IF-MAP and its acquisition of data helps to homogenize the data of arbitrary and different network components. The components must therefore only be extended to publish their information to the central MAP server (MAPS).

(2) *Data Context.* Using IF-MAPs *links* to connect information like network addresses, user credentials and services as well as (automatically) detected high-level events provides a benefit to the user, as this information has not to be connected manually from separate views in a graphical software or even different analysis tools.

(3) *Interoperability*. Another benefit by using IF-MAP as the underlying technique is the ability to use the proposed software tool VisITMeta in any network that facilitates an IF-MAP environment.

(4) *Continuous Recording and Retrospective Analysis*. By collecting all information and persisting them as they are processed by the MAPS, a retrospective analysis can be done, where even the differences in the graph between two given timestamps can be inspected. If something happened in the network, the changes in the state of all involved components can be reconstructed step by step in the same order as these changes were registered by the MAPS.

7.2   Identified Challenges

(1) *Visual Scalability*. Big graphs get cluttered really quick and loose the possible insight gain for the user. Techniques to reduce the size of the graph data shown to the user at a time have to be added to the visualization. Mechanisms like a level of detail approach, where parts of the graph were collapsed into single abstract nodes when zooming out would help retain the overall view on the graph.

(2) *Visual Dynamics*. Networks characterized by fast and frequent changes also lead to many changes in the visualization. This makes it difficult for the user to track single changes in a live view of the network. Besides from techniques on the visualization side to reduce the visual changes, an approach to reduce the incoming data could also be useful. By removing low-level data from the graph and relying on high-level data of detection components that abstract the low-level data could also lead to fewer but more meaningful changes in the visualized data.

(3) *Recording of All Data*. The mechanism to fetch the data from the MAPS has a basic shortcoming, as only connected graphs can be observed via the subscribe operation. Multiple subscriptions for every disconnected graph minimize the problem, but to get to know if there are (new) disconnected graphs not observed by running subscriptions is not supported via standard means by a MAPS.

8   Conclusion and Future Work

In this paper we have argued that an integrated and extensible monitoring system that gathers information from various network components is required to quickly and accurately detect and analyze security-related events. In the visualization of such integrated data, historical analysis and a suitable representation are needed to support a deeper understanding and invoke necessary measures. Thus we derived different requirements for a data model, its persistence and specifically its visualization. We presented IF-MAP as a suitable approach to integrate data from different heterogeneous data sources and extended its data model for the persistence of MAP graphs. Furthermore, we defined requirements regarding the visualization of such integrated data. Based on these requirements we have presented concepts for an advanced visualization component based on IF-MAP. Our prototypical implementation of these concepts, the software application VisITMeta, targets the requirements on two different levels, operating as a data repository and providing a useful visualization with the possibility for further extensions.

Future work in terms of extending the VisITMeta software include the implementation of multi-layouts allowing different layouts for subgraphs—e.g., by combining a force-directed algorithm for the overall layout with the bipartite layout for subgraphs—as well as mechanisms within the GUI to filter and search the displayed graphs with more options. Another field of work is to handle extremely large graphs in their visualization by abstracting groups of graph elements into single meta-nodes that can be expanded on demand by the user (generalization).

Beside the extension of VisITMeta as a tool itself, we are also looking towards its integration into a bigger environment. Although VisITMeta already allows for live and historical analysis of MAP data, it gets difficult to manually analyze and track the network state. Especially in larger scenarios the full graph becomes very complex and confusing. Time-critical decision making and the detection of complex scenarios therefore require an automated analysis of the integrated data. We pursue such an approach in another current research project[9]. Both aspects of the VisiITMeta application are continued to be used: the data persistence with its interface as input to a graph-pattern-based detection component as well as the visualization as an integrated tool in a SIEM-like GUI. The VisITMeta visualization can be utilized to take a detailed look at the graph state when incidents in the network were monitored. This allows for a focused analysis to gain a deeper understanding of smaller parts of the network (graph) and also allow for a retrospective auditing.

Acknowledgements. The fruitful collaboration with Gabi Dreo Rodosek, Josef von Helden, Frauke Sprengel, and our students is gratefully acknowledged. This work is financially supported by the German Federal Ministry of Education and Research (BMBF) within the projects VisITMeta (grant no. 17PNT032) and SIMU (grant no. 16KIS0045).

References

1. Ahlers, V., Heine, F., Hellmann, B., Kleiner, C., Renners, L., Rossow, T., Steuerwald, R.: Replicable security monitoring: Visualizing time-variant graphs of network metadata. In: CEUR Workshop Proceedings of the Joint Proceedings of the Fourth International Workshop on Euler Diagrams and the First International Workshop on Graph Visualization in Practice co-located with Diagrams, vol. 1244, pp. 32–41 (2014)
2. Bente, I., Hellmann, B., Vieweg, J., von Helden, J., Dreo, G.: TCADS: trustworthy, context-related anomaly detection for smartphones. In: Barolli, L., Taniar, D., Enokido, T., Rahayu, J.W., Takizawa, M. (eds.) 15th International Conference on Network-Based Information Systems, NBiS, pp. 247–254. IEEE (2012)

---

[9] http://simu-project.de/.

3. Birkholz, H., Sieverdingbeck, I., Sohr, K., Bormann, C.: IO: an interconnected asset ontology in support of risk management processes. In: Proceedings of the Seventh International Conference on Availability, Reliability and Security, ARES 2012, pp. 534–541. IEEE (2012)

4. Boschetti, A., Salgarelli, L., Muelder, C., Ma, K.-L.: TVi: a visual querying system for network monitoring and anomaly detection. In: Proceedings of the 8th International Symposium on Visualization for Cyber Security, VizSec 2011, pp. 1–10. ACM (2011)

5. Debar, H., Curry, D., Feinstein, B.: The intrusion detection message exchange format (IDMEF), RFC 4765 (Experimental), March 2007

6. Goodall, J., Sowul, M.: VIAssist: visual analytics for cyber defense. In: Proceedings of the IEEE Conference on Technologies for Homeland Security, HST 2009, pp. 143–150. IEEE (2009)

7. Karg, D., Muñoz, J.D., Gil, D., Ospitia, F., González, S., Casal, J.: OSSIM: open source security information management, general system description, version 0.18, November 2003. http://www.alienvault.com/docs/OSSIM-desc-en.pdf

8. Liao, Q., Blaich, A., Striegel, A., Thain, D.: ENAVis: enterprise network activities visualization. In: Proceedings of the 22nd Large Installation System Administration Conference, LISA, pp. 59–74. USENIX Association (2008)

9. Liao, Q., Striegel, A., Chawla, N.: Visualizing graph dynamics and similarity for enterprise network security and management. In: Proceedings of the Seventh International Symposium on Visualization for Cyber Security, VizSec 2010, pp. 34–45. ACM (2010)

10. Novikova, E., Kotenko, I.: Analytical visualization techniques for security information and event management. In: 21st Euromicro International Conference on Parallel, Distributed, and Network-Based Processing, PDP, pp. 519–525. IEEE Computer Society Press (2013)

11. Tamassia, R., Palazzi, B., Papamanthou, C.: Graph drawing for security visualization. In: Tollis, I.G., Patrignani, M. (eds.) GD 2008. LNCS, vol. 5417, pp. 2–13. Springer, Heidelberg (2009)

12. Trusted Network Connect Working Group. TNC IF-MAP binding for SOAP, version 2.1, Revision 15, May 2012. http://www.trustedcomputinggroup.org/resources/tnc_ifmap_binding_for_soap_specification

13. Trusted Network Connect Working Group. TNC IF-MAP metadata for network security, version 1.1, Revision 8, May 2012. http://www.trustedcomputinggroup.org/resources/tnc_ifmap_metadata_for_network_security

14. Yasm, C.: Prelude as a hybrid IDS framework. Technical report, SAMS Institute (2009). http://www.sans.org/reading-room/whitepapers/awareness/prelude-hybrid-ids-framework-33048

SysML-Sec Attack Graphs: Compact Representations for Complex Attacks

Ludovic Apvrille[1]([✉]) and Yves Roudier[2]

[1] Institut Mines-Telecom, Telecom ParisTech, CNRS LTCI,
Sophia Antipolis, France
ludovic.apvrille@telecom-paristech.fr
[2] EURECOM, Sophia Antipolis, France
yves.roudier@eurecom.fr

Abstract. We discuss in this paper the use of SysML-Sec attack graphs as a graphical and semi-formal representation for complex attacks. We illustrate this on a PC and mobile malware example. We furthermore provide examples of the expressivity of the operators used in such diagrams. We finally formalize the attack traces described by these operators based on timed automata.

1 Introduction

Modeling security threats in distributed systems, and even more so in embedded system is a usual aspect of the work of security analysts. However, more than often, the threat analysis simply relies on the knowledge of specific malware and their variants, or on the exploitation of well-known vulnerabilities rather than in finding new combinations of attacks.

Unfortunately, an increasing number of embedded systems have become communicating artifacts, feature new interactions with their immediate environment or with backend systems, and are thus exposed to criminals. Many of these security issues reflect either the exploitation of low-level vulnerabilities, which might often be addressed with appropriate programming practices and specific component tests, or design flaws due to an insufficient understanding of the mapping of functional or security logical components to the hardware architecture.

We introduced in the SysML-Sec framework [2] a more systematic representation of attacks envisioned or known to be feasible on the system under design and/or development. In the framework of the activities undertaken when following a Model-Driven Engineering (MDE) approach, the attack modeling phase is known as a very important driver for motivating the need for introducing security countermeasures in a risk analysis, and also for selecting where those security mechanisms better fit.

SysML-Sec extends SysML's parametric diagram in order to depict attacks, their composition, and to represent the assets target of these attacks in an attack graph. We also discuss in this paper the use of attack graphs and their operators and define their formal semantics based on timed automata (novel contribution). We also introduce a more complete example of application of such an analysis to model the Zeus/Zitmo mobile malware that were not published before.

© Springer International Publishing Switzerland 2016
S. Mauw et al. (Eds.): GraMSec 2015, LNCS 9390, pp. 35–49, 2016.
DOI: 10.1007/978-3-319-29968-6_3

2   Attack Modeling

Threats and Attacks. Threats and security vulnerabilities of the selected assets should as much as possible describe the capabilities that an attacker should meet or exceed and the origin of attacks (local, remote, through a specific interface). The SysML-Sec environment supports the assessment of risks following the approach described in more detail in the EVITA case study [8,13]. We also implemented automated checks of the threat coverage by security objectives. Based on the risk analysis, one should also identify and prioritize security objectives that are mapped to a threat.

Attack Graphs. Instead of using the traditional attack tree approach [14], we suggest that threats can be better modeled with a more relational approach, using slightly customized SysML Parametric Diagrams. Threats are modeled as values embedded into blocks representing the target of the attacks, thus achieving a representation that visually emphasizes the assets. Attacks ($<< attack >>$ stereotype) can be linked together with a few primitive operators. Those operators are either logical operators like AND, OR, and XOR, or temporal causality operators like $SEQUENCE$, $BEFORE$, or $AFTER$. We consider the latter constructs as especially helpful to describe the attacker's operational point of view in embedded systems, like for instance situations in which there is a maximum duration between two causally related attacks. For example, when attacking a system with time-limited authentication tokens, the token must be first retrieved, and then the use of this token must occur before its expiration.

Attack instances in different parametric diagrams can be linked together in order to assess the impact of a specific vulnerability and the need to address it at the risk assessment phase. An attack can also be tagged as a *root* attack, meaning that this attack is at the top of a tree of attacks. In other words, such an attack is not used to built up more complex attacks. Last but not least, attacks can be linked to requirements, thus allowing an automated check of the coverage of attacks by verifying whether each attack is linked to at least one security requirement.

The attacks in multiple diagrams finally result in a directed graph whose vertices can be either individual attacks (or leaf attacks), intermediate attacks (resulting from the composition of multiple other attacks), or operators that combine other attacks. We currently only consider acyclic graphs, but we are currently considering an extension to cyclic graphs in order to model resource usage (see the discussion in Sect. 6). Last but not least, we do not claim that these operators are always well adapted for modeling attack graphs, but at least, attack graphs offers a richer semantics than the one of attack trees, thus leading to more compact representations (in other words: less operators must be used). Also, attacks graphs demonstrated their ability to model complex attack scenarios, e.g. Zeus/Zitmo.

3   Example: Modeling Zeus/Zitmo

The Mobile component of the ZeuS crimeware kit (also known as or Trojan-Spy.*.Zitmo) was released in 2010 in order to intercept mobile Transaction Authentication Numbers ($mTAN$ codes) from mobile phones.

The PC/Windows component, Zeus, modifies the browser of Microsoft Windows computers with a malicious plugin, so that any attempt to access an online bank website redirects the request to a fake bank site provided by the attacker. Additionaly, a keylogger spies username/password pairs to make it possible for the attacker to log undetected into the real banking system of the user. Zitmo also maliciously suggests the user to install a fake mobile bank application on his/her mobile phone. Once done, the fake application spies received SMS messages so as to silently steal mTANs.

The SysML-Sec attack graph of this trojan is given in Fig. 1. It has been made with TTool [1]. The system attacker is modeled with two main sub-blocks: the attacker PC that is used to gather information on users credentials (username,

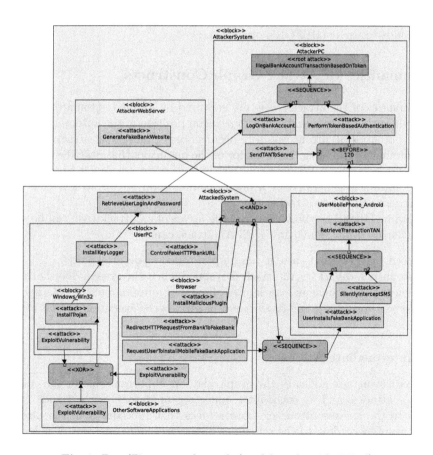

Fig. 1. Zeus/Zitmo attack graph (model made with TTool)

password, mTAN) and to perform illegal transactions using those credentials, and a webserver used to host fake bank websites. The attacked system consists in both the Windows PC of the targeted person, and his/her Android mobile phone. The first exploit is performed on the Windows PC, either using a Win32 exploit, or a browser exploit, or using other exploits in applications: the attack graph model thus contains three sub-blocks in the "UserPC" block. The XOR operator expresses that as soon as one exploit was performed on the targeted PC, the trojan can be installed and no further exploit linked to the XOR is useful. The trojan intercepts the username and password of the user, and sends them back to the attacker system. In parallel, several attacks are necessary in order to intercept requests to the bank system: the attacker must settle a fake bank server. The attacker must also control the *http* request to the bank system. He/She also has to install a malicious plugin in the browser of the attacked PC. Once all this has been done (AND operator), the browser can ask the user to install a fake Android application on his/her mobile phone (SEQUENCE operator in the bottom right part of the model). Once installed, the fake application can silently monitor SMS (SEQUENCE operator in the "UserMobilePhone_Android" block), and thus retrieve *mTANs*. When an mTAN has been obtained, the attacker has 120 seconds to use it (BEFORE operator).

4   Semantics of Attack Graph Constructs

The semantics of the attack traces are captured by a timed automaton which is the result of the parallel and synchronized composition of the automata expressing the potential occurrences and re-occurrences of individual attacks together with automata expressing the behavior of the operators that describe how these attacks are composed. Without any loss of generality, we depict in the following the automata generated by a binary combination of two attacks (but they support more than two attacks).

Individual attacks, which would be the leaves of an attack tree, can be modeled as depicted for *attack1* in Fig. 2. An attack can:

- Succeed (*a1!*). In that case, it can be performed again afterwards.
- Be stopped (*stop_a1?*). An attack is stopped when the system does not allow the activation of such an attack after all related automata of the attack graph are synchronized, e.g., an XOR operator forbids the execution of that attack.

4.1   Intermediate Attacks

Intermediate attack nodes in the graph play an important role in the composition of attacks, and as such, interconnecting operators. Such a node corresponds to the success of one or more attacks that precedes it in the directed attack graph according to the semantics of the preceding operator. The semantics of those nodes must more specifically support the backward propagation of *stop* events within the graph. Thus, an intermediate attack (see Fig. 3) first

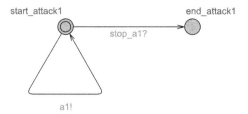

Fig. 2. Semantics of an individual attack

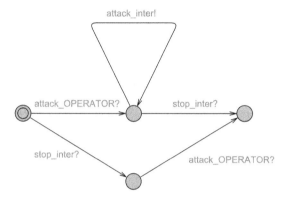

Fig. 3. Semantics of an intermediate attack node

waits for its activation operator (*attack_OPERATOR*), then, it can be executed several times (*attack_inter*), or be stopped (*stop_inter*). Also, before its activation operator is complete, it can be stopped ((*stop_inter* from the initial state): in that latter case, only the completion of its operator can be performed (*attack_OPERATOR*).

Finally, we assume that an oriented connection between attacks *attack1* to *attack2* is a shortcut for *attack1* to an OR node, and then from the OR node to *attack2*.

4.2 And Operator

The AND operator models the expectation that multiple attacks are required to be executed in conjunction (possibly in a parallel fashion). Failing to achieve any of the elementary attacks results in the overall failure of subsequent dependent attacks. For instance, many malware rely on checks to make sure they are not running in a virtualized honeypot: all those checks should succeed and thus can be modelled as attacks under an AND.

The timed automaton formalizing the behavior of the operator is depicted in Fig. 4. It performs the synchronization of the automata of the underlying attacks. The handling of an additional attack would result in an additional transition at the second state of this timed automaton.

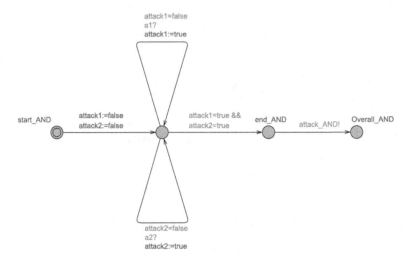

Fig. 4. AND operator

4.3   Or Operator

The OR operator models a situation in which multiple attacks can be executed to enable other composite attacks. The first successful attack will enable the execution of new composite attacks farther in the attack graph. Also not all attacks under the OR operator need to be performed before a composite attack using the OR proceeds or even succeeds (see Fig. 5).

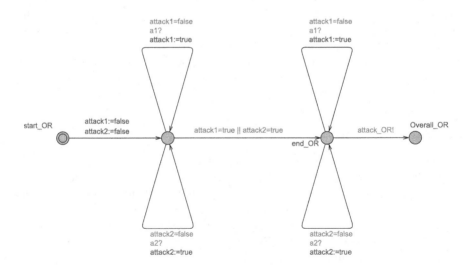

Fig. 5. OR operator

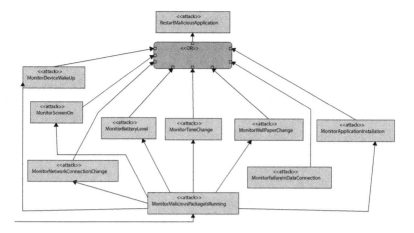

Fig. 6. OR operator - Excerpt of the attack graph of Chuli

This operator can for instance model redundant operations that an attacker or a malware may perform for instance to extract some information.

Let's take the example of an OR operator taken from the model of the Chuli Android mobile malware [7]. Basically, Chuli infects mobile phones through spam emails, and then sends to the remote attacker's server private information contained on the mobile phone. One interesting feature of this malware is its ability to monitor whether it is running or not using callback services triggered by external events, e.g., *ScreenOn* and *BatteryLevel* events. As soon as one of this event occurs in the system, Chuli can restart its main application, if necessary. Thus, all those trigger events can be monitored in parallel. Said differently, one among all events is enough for Chuli to perform the check. Also, once one event has been used by Chuli, Chuli continues other events. All this corresponds to an OR operator, see Fig. 6.

4.4   XOR Operator

The XOR operator models alternative and exclusive independent attacks. Thus, the behavior of interest expressed by this operator is the success of a single attack. Said differently, any first successful attack among those referenced by the operator is the one that will appear in the trace of the attack at the exclusion of all others.

The semantics with OR is different because an XOR forbids the execution of other attacks, apart form the first successful one. On the contrary, OR does not impose any constraint on other attacks. For example, in a situation in which attacks are tested in parallel - for example, a monitor waiting for several callbacks informing about a success -, then the OR operator shall be used. In a situation where only one of the attack is tested, one after the other, without imposing the order of testing, then, the XOR operator shall be used.

More formally (see Fig. 7), once one attacks has been successfully performed (*a*1? or *a*2?), the attack that was not performed is deactivated (*stop_a*1! or *stop_a*2!), and then the intermediate attack is executed (*attack_XOR*).

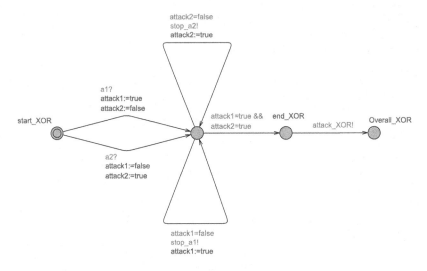

Fig. 7. XOR operator

4.5   SEQUENCE Operator

The SEQUENCE operator models attacks which must be performed in a strict order $a_1, a_2, ...; a_n$ (see Fig. 8). Failing to achieve one attack a_i makes it impossible to subsequently execute attacks a_j with $j > i$.

Fig. 8. Sequence operator

4.6   BEFORE Operator

The BEFORE operators is based on a sequence of attacks with a **maximum** duration between two consecutive attacks (see Fig. 9). Just like for the SEQUENCE, failing to achieve one attacks makes it impossible to achieve subsequent attacks. Moreover, failing to achieve one attack within its given allowed period of execution also makes it impossible to execute subsequent attacks.

This operator is particularly suited to model life-time limited tokens.

Fig. 9. Before operator

4.7 AFTER Operator

The AFTER operators is based on a sequence of attacks with a **minimum** duration between two consecutive attacks (see Fig. 10). Just like for the SEQUENCE, failing to achieve one attacks makes it impossible to achieve subsequent attacks. Moreover, if an attack is available for execution before the minimum duration, the system will force it to execute only after the minimum duration.

The AFTER operator is particularly interesting to model situations in which an attack is useless before waiting for an access to be available, e.g., when brute-forcing a password system with a minimum delay between two attempts.

Fig. 10. After operator

5 System Validation

From a formal verification perspective, attack graphs can be formally analyzed directly from TTool, in terms of reachability, liveness and "leads to" properties on attacks.

- Reachability of an attack a. Means that there exists at least one possible series of attacks $a_1, a_2, ..., a_n, a$ (i.e., trace of attacks) that leads to a.
- Liveness of an attack a. Means that whatever the possible traces of attacks in the system $a_1, a_2, ...; a_n, \exists i/a_i = a$.
- Liveness of an attack b after another attack a was performed. Means that whenever a trace of attacks contains $a = a_i : a_1, a_2, ...; a_n, \exists j > i/a_j = b$. This property is commonly named "leads to" (this is the case in TTool) or also "response".

From SysML-Sec models edited in TTool, a user can either simulate the model, or perform formal proofs with UPPAAL [3]. The simulation engine integrated in TTool allows usual commands (step-by-step execution, reaching next breakpoint, etc.), and animates the attack graph while it is simulated. A sequence diagram representing the trace of performed attacks is displayed as well. Formal proofs can also be performed with a press-button approach directly from TTool (but UPPAAL needs to be installed): indeed, TTool automatically transforms

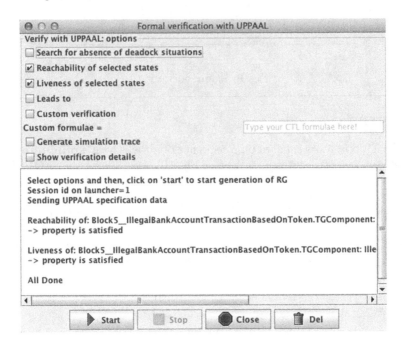

Fig. 11. Reachability and liveness of the main attack (TTool dialog window)

Leads to: RedirectHTTPRequestFromBankToFakeBank--> IllegalBankAccountTransactionBasedOnToken
-> property is satisfied

Leads to: IllegalBankAccountTransactionBasedOnToken--> RedirectHTTPRequestFromBankToFakeBank
-> property is NOT satisfied

Fig. 12. "Leads to" property proved from TTool

the attack graphs into a UPPAAL specification, feeds it into UPPAAL, gets the results, and presents them in a friendly way. This model transformation is instantaneous from a user's perspective in all case studies we've made (linear algorithm). The formal proof complexity obviously depends on the model concurrency, e.g., the use of OR operators increases the concurrency, whereas the use of SEQUENCE constraints traces.

Figure 11 displays the reachability and liveness dialog window of TTool for the "root attack" ("IllegalBankAccountTransactionBasedOnToken") of the Zitmo model (Fig. 1). Both the reachability and liveness are satisfied.

A "leads to" property can be evaluated if two attacks have been selected. For instance, in the Zitmo model (Fig. 1), we can select the two attacks a_1 = "RedirectHttpRequestFromBankToFakeBank" and a_2 = "IllegalBankAccounttransactionBasedOnToken" (see Fig. 12): The "leads to" property holds for $a_1 \rightsquigarrow a_2$ but not for $a_2 \rightsquigarrow a_1$.

TTool also allows to enable/disable attacks of attacks trees, so as to understand what is the importance/impact of an attack on the system. For example,

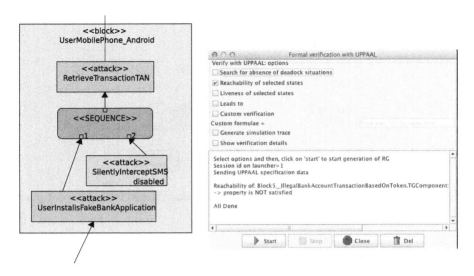

Fig. 13. An attack has been disabled in the Zitmo attack graph (Diagram on the left). Because of the disabled attack, the root attack cannot be performed anymore (right part of the figure).

if we disable the attack "SilentlyInterceptSMS" (left part of Fig. 13), then, the root attack is not reachable anymore (right part of Fig. 13).

6 Combining Operators and Attacks

This section discusses ways to handle complex attack relations relying on the relations between attacks described in Sect. 4.

6.1 Prioritizing Attacks Under a XOR

The XOR operator imposes no priority on the execution of the possible attacks. However, such an order may be achieved by combining an XOR with all the acceptable orderings of individual attacks, as can be described using the SEQ operator. Such a composite operator can be implemented based on the operators described above but requires generating all possible interleavings. To simplify the specification, we suggest the definition of a macro operator, SXOR. Such a macro operator could be integrated in the TTool environment. In the longer term, if such operators would prove useful, they may be standardized as a library shared by all SysML-Sec designers.

6.2 Compatibility Between Temporal Constraints

The joint use of AFTER and BEFORE can lead to situations where attacks are not reachable, because of the timing values of these operators. For example,

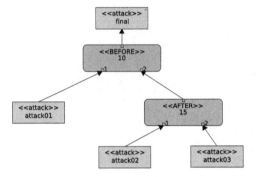

Fig. 14. The "final" attack cannot be performed because the two temporal constraints are not compatible

in Fig. 14, the root attack is not reachable because an attack is required to be performed before 10 units of time. But the AFTER operator forbids that situation. Modifying the temporal value in AFTER and BEFORE can make the root attack reachable, for example, by using the same temporal value. TTool can already analyze such situations, i.e., it can identify non reachable attacks because of non compatible timing constraints.

6.3   Cycles and Reachability

Cycles can be obtained in attack graphs by linking an attack generated from an operator to operators that were already handled previously in the trace of attacks.

For example, if we consider Fig. 15, *rootattack2* is reachable because the cycle occurs on a OR operator. If the same cycle is performed on the AND operator, then, the latter can never be executed, and so, *rootattack1* is not reachable.

Currently, such a situation is not supported by TTool, and by our semantics. A finer control over the use of cycles in general will require defining how many executions of the same operator can be allowed, for instance by adding

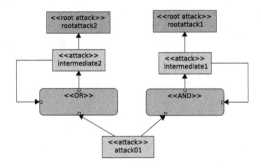

Fig. 15. Cycles. rootattack2 is reachable, but not rootattack1

an execution counter on each operator. Similarly, as long as they have not been explicitly stopped, attacks can be performed an infinite number of times: counters should also be added to these constructs. This work should be especially useful in the face of the modeling of denial of service attacks, which require not only a qualitative, but a quantitative assessment of the attacker's capabilities. We plan to develop these techniques as part of our future work.

7 Related Work and Perspectives

The formalism of attack trees brought to light by [14] has long been used to describe threats to applications and systems, and attacks to implement those threats. In that respect, attack trees are closely related to fault trees in dependable computing. Attack trees follow a goal-oriented approach that matches the objectives of an attacker and roughly describes an attack trace. However they capture a unique trace, and make it hard capturing complex attack scenarios built upon sub-attacks. They also fail at capturing the architectural components involved in a given attack with regards to the assets under attack, even though this often constitutes an important information for the trustfulness one can put into a component. In our case, location of attacks are given by their mapping onto architectural components.

Multiple variants of attack trees have been developed: they introduced operators with increasingly advanced semantics, e.g., [10], yet that have not addressed the above-mentioned issues. Our work tries to address these concerns based on the structure of our attack graphs rather than based only on the operators themselves. Among other benefits, this structure simplifies the reuse of sub-attacks without any duplication.

Attack graphs have been proposed and formalized even before attack trees received a widespread audience, like for instance privilege graphs [5], and more recently in order to automatically generate them from other formalisms [15]. [5] particular emphasized the quantitative aspect of the security assessment of threats. A Markovian model was used to determine the privileged edges in an attack graph. Our work also aims to introduce quantitative assessments while still retaining the hierarchical modeling that made the success of attack trees, and which is also connected with the system architecture in SysML-Sec in contrast with the "maze" graph described by the authors of [5].

Extensions were suggested to complement the static attack tree representations with more dynamic models. For instance, Petri net based approaches [6,12] were proposed in order to describe the triggering of different phases of an attack within an attack tree. [11] also suggested the use of Markovian processes (BDMP) to describe relationships between different attacks organized in a tree-like fashion but whose triggering could be independent from that structure. More recently, [16] relies on attack trees to complement the static analysis and dynamic analysis of Android malware: Nodes are enriched with e.g., permissions and capabilities ("P": Possible to realize; "I": impossible to realize). Other formalisms than attack trees have been introduced in order to capture attacks, but they are generally targeting security mechanisms first. We can mention modeling environments such as UMLSec [9], and tools for the proof of security properties in security protocols [4].

In a way, all these models also describe attack graphs with edges corresponding to different relationships. However, the approach described in this paper mostly focuses on expressing multiple attack traces. It aims at understanding whether a system is vulnerable and thus help deciding which security counter-measures might be most important through attack reachability and liveness analyses. Indeed, TTool facilitates the activation/deactivation of attacks in the graph, thus allowing to analyze the reachability and liveness of attacks in different situations. Combined with the location of attacks, this helps determining which and where attacks should be addressed first. We also believe that the modeling of our phases is more straightforward than the approaches we just outlined, because it is more rich w.r.t. attack trees, and more prone to the modular expression of threats due to the asset-centric distribution of attacks.

8   Conclusion and Future Work

From our experience, partitioning is a very important element when modeling attacks in order to understand both the assets at risk, their potential vulnerabilities, as well as the capabilities of the attacker. Thus, SysML-Sec proposes to use iterations between security requirements, attack graphs and partitioning models. Attack graphs adopt a block-centric perspective with reuse in mind. We especially think that this will allow for the composition of the threat modeling performed by security analysts about components over-the-shelf (COTS) with system specific analyses.

A few extensions of our work have already been discussed in Sect. 6. We plan to further extend SysML-Sec expressivity as follows: our declarative approach should be especially useful in order to incorporate knowledge from other threat modeling approaches. In that respect, our proposal explicitly maps attacks to the architecture, and makes it possible to introduce an abstract model of the attacker within the SysML parametric diagram for threat modeling. We essentially plan to extend our approach towards more quantitative assessments of threats, and also to integrate together attack graphs and risk assessment, e.g., using risk values on edges between attacks and operators.

References

1. Apvrille, L.: TTool website (2013). http://ttool.telecom-paristech.fr/
2. Apvrille, L., Roudier, Y.: SysML-sec: a sysML environment for the design and development of secure embedded systems. In: APCOSEC , Asia-Pacific Council on Systems Engineering, 8–11 September 2013, Yokohama, Japan. Yokohama, JAPAN (09 2013) (2013). http://www.eurecom.fr/publication/4186
3. Bengtsson, J.E., Yi, W.: Timed automata: semantics, algorithms and tools. In: Desel, J., Reisig, W., Rozenberg, G. (eds.) Lectures on Concurrency and Petri Nets. LNCS, vol. 3098, pp. 87–124. Springer, Heidelberg (2004)

4. Blanchet, B.: Automatic verification of correspondences for security protocols. J. Comput. Secur. **17**(4), 363–434 (2009)
5. Dacier, M., Deswarte, Y., Kaâniche, M.: Information systems security, pp. 177–186. Chapman & Hall Ltd, London, UK (1996). http://dl.acm.org/citation.cfm?id=265514.265530
6. Dalton, G., Mills, R., Colombi, J., Raines, R.: Analyzing attack trees using generalized stochastic petri nets. In: Information Assurance Workshop, 2006 IEEE, pp. 116–123, June 2006
7. Fortinet: The Android/Chuli.A!tr.spy virus, March 2013. http://www.fortiguard.com/encyclopedia/virus/#id=4805535
8. Henniger, O., Apvrille, L., Fuchs, A., Roudier, Y., Ruddle, A., Weyl, B.: Security requirements for automotive on-board networks. In: ITST, Lille, France (2009)
9. Jürjens, J.: UMLsec: extending UML for secure systems development. In: Jézéquel, J.-M., Hussmann, H., Cook, S. (eds.) UML 2002. LNCS, vol. 2460, pp. 412–425. Springer, Heidelberg (2002)
10. Khand, P.: System level security modeling using attack trees. In: 2nd International Conference on Computer, Control and Communication, 2009. IC4 2009, pp. 1–6, February 2009
11. Piètre-Cambacédès, L., Bouissou, M.: Beyond attack trees: dynamic security modeling with Boolean logic driven markov processes (bdmp). In: Dependable Computing Conference (EDCC), 2010 European, pp. 199–208, April 2010
12. Pudar, S., Manimaran, G., Liu, C.C.: Penet: a practical method and tool for integrated modeling of security attacks and countermeasures. Comput. Secur. **28**(8), 754–771 (2009). http://www.sciencedirect.com/science/article/pii/S0167404809000522
13. Ruddle, A., et al.: Security Requirements for Automotive On-board Networks Based on Dark-side Scenarios. Technical report. Deliverable D2.3, EVITA Project (2009)
14. Schneier, B.: Attack Trees: Modeling Security Threats, December 1999
15. Vigo, R., Nielson, F., Nielson, H.: Automated generation of attack trees. In: 2014 IEEE 27th Computer Security Foundations Symposium (CSF), pp. 337–350, July 2014
16. Zhao, S., Li, X., Xu, G., Zhang, L., Feng, Z.: Attack tree based android malware detection with hybrid analysis. In: IEEE 13th International Conference on Trust, Security and Privacy in Computing and Communications (TrustCom), pp. 380–387, September 2014

How to Generate Security Cameras: Towards Defence Generation for Socio-Technical Systems

Olga Gadyatskaya[✉]

SnT, University of Luxembourg, Luxembourg City, Luxembourg
olga.gadyatskaya@uni.lu

Abstract. Recently security researchers have started to look into automated generation of attack trees from socio-technical system models. The obvious next step in this trend of automated risk analysis is automating the selection of security controls to treat the detected threats. However, the existing socio-technical models are too abstract to represent all security controls recommended by practitioners and standards. In this paper we propose an attack-defence model, consisting of a set of attack-defence bundles, to be generated and maintained with the socio-technical model. The attack-defence bundles can be used to synthesise attack-defence trees directly from the model to offer basic attack-defence analysis, but also they can be used to select and maintain the security controls that cannot be handled by the model itself.

Keywords: Attack-defence trees · Socio-technical models · Generation of attack models · Generation of defences

1 Introduction

Models are used in all stages of the security process: from security requirements elicitation and organisational risk assessment to run-time verification and business process compliance audit. Often these models are inter-connected. For example, if a security requirements model for a software system was elicited, on the later stage it may be re-used to design the security testing process for this system. At the same time, as manual production of security models is very tedious and error-prone, many researchers and practitioners look into automating the model creation and transformation processes.

Recently security researchers have looked at systematic design [15] and automated generation of attack models [7,8,14,22], such as attack graphs and attack trees, from system models. This model transformation allows to switch the view from the system description perspective to a compact representation of possible attacker actions. At the same time, given the generated attack model, the system defender is interested to find the weakest links: the spots in the model where additional security controls can be introduced to improve protection and eliminate potential attacks. Therefore, automated generation of defences is an obvious next step in the process.

© Springer International Publishing Switzerland 2016
S. Mauw et al. (Eds.): GraMSec 2015, LNCS 9390, pp. 50–65, 2016.
DOI: 10.1007/978-3-319-29968-6_4

In this paper we look at socio-technical models as succinct abstractions of large organisations. Such models capture simultaneously locations, actors and objects in the system. They often take into account both physical and digital domains and offer to a human analyst the means to represent "the world as it is". That means that the designer of socio-technical systems does not need to be a security or risk analysis expert. She only needs to know the intricacies of her own company (department) to be able to model it. With the system model at hand, at the next step the attack generation tools aim at automatic creation of attack scenarios that can be further discussed by security professionals. The overall idea of this process is to automate threat scenarios identification (an important aspect of risk analysis) as much as possible.

In this paper we would like to push the envelope even further. Our main question is: *given a socio-technical system model, how to find and capture, possibly automatically, the security controls that will counteract the discovered threats?* Indeed, the main goal of risk analysis is to improve the existing system by introducing new security controls, so that the most dangerous or easily executed attacks are thwarted. Therefore, automated creation of attack scenarios only is not yet a full solution.

We want to look at perspectives and limitations of automated defence generation from socio-technical models. It seems that the main obstacle to rich defensive strategies generation directly from the model is the fact that socio-technical models do not capture many security controls.

To find an answer to the main question, we start from investigating the security controls (defences) already present in an advanced socio-technical model and propose a scheme to extract these controls, together with the attack steps, in the compact format of attack-defence bundles. We then evaluate the limitations of the extracted defences inherent from the socio-technical model and discuss how to overcome these limitations. We argue that an attack-defence model needs to be maintained (in parallel with the socio-technical model) that can capture not only the attacker's view but also the defender's view of the system. In this paper we have chosen attack-defence trees [11] as the basis for the attack-defence model. As an alternative to this model, one can choose, for example, attack-countermeasure trees [20].

The goal of this paper is to propose an attack-defence view for socio-technical models that can capture simultaneously attacker's options and available/proposed countermeasures in the system. The main idea is that given that view it can be easily synchronised with the model (but it contains richer defence information than the model), and it can be used to synthesise attack-defence trees and evaluate different interesting attributes.

2   Socio-Technical Models Versus Attack-Defence Models

As socio-technical models are abstractions, they do not capture all defensive mechanisms that can be available in an organisation, but only a subset of them. Indeed, it is impossible to model all security-relevant devices, protocols and behaviours in a single model. Typically, socio-technical models look at capturing organisational infrastructure (e.g., [10,12,16,18]), but sometimes they can focus only on some aspects of human-computer interactions (e.g., [6,19]).

Since all security aspects cannot be captured by a socio-technical model without overcomplicating it, we argue that there is a need to maintain a separate view of attack and defence capabilities of the system together with the socio-technical model. Preferably, we should be able to trace the objects in the socio-technical model into the attack-defence model and back.

Requirements for the Attack-Defence Model. The first requirement for the chosen attack-defence model is that *the defences that are already captured by the model need to be represented explicitly in the attack-defence model*. Indeed, we would like to faithfully represent the system security state. So, if some security control is captured by the system model, it should be translated into the generated attack-defence model.

Secondly, we want to propose a way to *update the generated defender's view (the security controls obtained directly from the system model) with more security controls and countermeasures* of the organisation. This *update needs to be consistent*: once a security control is captured in the attack-defence model, it should be traced to an object in the system model. For example, if our approach identifies that a security camera is to be placed in a certain location in the system, all attack scenarios that involve that location should be updated to take the camera into account. In this way later on one can investigate automated defence generation process that will maintain consistency of the socio-technical system.

Background. In this paper we use the TREsPASS socio-technical model [10] that is graph-based. We can briefly summarise this model as follows. Locations in the system represent physical and network locations; actors model humans and processes; and items can be physical or digital objects. Edges among locations represent connectedness (e.g., adjacent rooms), and all actors and items are located somewhere in the system. Actors can possess items, and items can be embedded into other items. Some locations have access control policies attached to them. These policies specify a set of credentials (items in the system) an actor needs to possess to enter the location or access the object. These policies can also be formalized by more complex predicates capturing, e.g., role-based access control or trust relationships among actors.

As the starting point for the attack-defence model, we consider the process of attack trees generation by policy invalidation that relies on structural information about the system [7–9]. This process was initially designed for the TREsPASS socio-technical model [10], but it can be applied to other socio-technical models capturing systems as graphs, e.g., [5,12,16,18], because it is reachability-based.

In short, this process is started by choosing an asset among the entities in the system. The attacker is also selected among actors in the system (the main goal of the attacker is to invalidate the security policy, e.g., confidentiality or integrity policy, associated with this asset). Then, based on the reachability reasoning, the process systematically searches for the ways for the attacker to access the asset. For example, consider the asset to be a sensitive document located in a locker in the manager's office, and the attacker to be an insider (an employee) working on the same floor. To access the document, the attacker can try to access the locker and open it (an AND-decomposition [11]). This might require possession of the key to the locker that needs to be obtained elsewhere in the system. Alternatively (an OR-decomposition with the previous attack), also the manager has access to the locker and the document. Thus, the attacker can get access the document by influencing the manager. This can be implemented through, e.g., social engineering (for instance, befriending the manager, or hiring an external actor to pretend to be a higher executive who needs the document), bribing, or coercing the manager.

In this small motivating example we see that two general attack strategies come into play: the attacker can actively pursue moving across the system and collecting items that will open him the way to the desired asset, or the attacker can attempt to orchestrate actions of other actors in the model so that they will do the necessary actions for him. Irrespectively of the chosen strategy, the process of attack trees generation by policy invalidation will systematically identify available (reachable) steps, add them to the tree, and refine those steps further, producing a complete attack tree in the end [8]. Notice, that this summary is a simplification of the overall process, and we encourage the reader to refer to the original articles about the approach for more details [7–9].

3   Attack-Defence Model

Extraction of Defences from the Model. The only security controls the TREsPASS socio-technical model captures are access control policies that restrict access to certain locations. These policies can correspond to physical (locks) or digital (password check) means (policy enforcement mechanisms) implemented in the system to restrict access to assets. Therefore, we propose to make explicit in the attack generation process the fact that the attacker needs to overcome the restrictions imposed by security policies. To achieve that we will use attack-defence bundles that are based on the attack-defence tree formalism [11].

Intuitively, the attacker can chose from two approaches to deal with security policies in the system. He can attempt to satisfy the access control policy (for example, by collecting the necessary credentials or coercing someone with the right credentials) or he can try to circumvent the policy (e.g., by forcing the lock). The first approach is in line with the attack tree generation by policy invalidation process, because it can be automatically designed based on reachability. If we want to refine the second approach, we need to understand how exactly different policies (more precisely – enforcement mechanisms for these policies) can be circumvented. There is a need to represent the human expert knowledge in circumventing different security mechanism in such a way that it is useful for automated generation process. To achieve that, one can use, for example, the hierarchical approach to attack representation suggested in [17].

Indeed, the enforcement mechanisms for access control policies defined in the socio-technical model can be automatically introduced into attack-defence trees. If the knowledge about breaking certain kinds of enforcement mechanisms is available in a suitable format (e.g., the hierarchical representation), then the attack-defence trees can be further refined based on that information. Further analysis based on the attack-defence trees produced at this stage (e.g., computation of the most probable or the most cheap attack for the attacker [4]) can identify the missing enforcement mechanisms. For example, if in the sensitive document scenario the attacker can directly access the document because the locker does not require any key (no access control is enforced for the document), it might be the first recommendation for improving security of the organisation: to introduce some appropriate access control mechanism (e.g., an actual lock with the key) to protect access to the document.

3.1   Simplified Socio-Technical Model

We introduce a simplified TREsPASS socio-technical model to exemplify the attack-defence model creation. The simplified model allows to reason only about potential reachability. However, this is already very useful for risk analysis, as quantitative evaluation of the possibility that an attacker accesses some system elements can simplify risk analysis for human analysts [13].

The simplified model captures simultaneously organisation's infrastructure topology for both physical and digital locations, as well as actors moving around this infrastructure (these can be persons or processes). In the model these entities are represented as a set of model elements N that is a union of a set of infrastructure locations N_i, actors N_a, and objects N_o. We consider two domains: Ph is the physical space (model elements in this domain are physical entities, including, e.g. rooms, persons, and items), while Dg is the digital space (network locations and processes are in this domain), such that $N = Ph \cup Dg$, and $Ph \cap Dg = \emptyset$.

Some model elements are connected. We denote as $E \subseteq N \times N$ the set of directed connections. All edges e in E are of the following types:

- $e \in E_{ii} \subseteq N_i \times N_i$: connections between infrastructure locations (rooms, corridors, etc.). These connections are assumed bi-directional. More precisely, if $(i_1, i_2) \in E_{ii}$ then $(i_2, i_1) \in E_{ii}$.
- $e \in E_{ai} \subseteq N_a \times N_i$: placement of actors in the infrastructure;
- $e \in E_{oi} \subseteq N_o \times N_i$: placement of objects in the infrastructure;
- $e \in E_{oa} \subseteq N_o \times N_a$: placement of objects that are carried around by actors;
- $e \in E_{oo} \subseteq N_o \times N_o$: placement of objects that are inside other objects; here $e = (o_1, o_2)$ denotes an object o_1 located within an object o_2.

Mutual intersections of $E_{ii}, E_{ai}, E_{oi}, E_{oa}, E_{oo}$ are empty sets. Elements of the same domain can be connected liberally. However, some self-evident restrictions apply when connections between elements of the physical and digital domains are considered. For example, a data file cannot be located in an office or inside a cupboard. We allow multiple locations for the same actor and object.

This corresponds to the possibility of actors to move in the model, and represents that some items can appear in several locations.

We define a location function $\texttt{loc}()$: $N \times N$ as follows: $\forall n \in N \; \texttt{loc}(n)$: $= \{l \in N | (n, l) \in E\}$.

Notice that for infrastructure locations or actors the function $\texttt{loc}()$ returns infrastructure locations where these model items are accessible from. However, as objects can be accessible from actors or other objects, $\texttt{loc}()$ may return any type of items in the model.

Policies. Let P be a set of policies defined in the model. We consider access control policies represented as tuples restricting access to element n. The *local policy* δ_n is a set of individual access control configurations. Each access control configuration $p \in \delta_n$ is a tuple $\langle Cred, atLocation, EM \rangle$, where $Cred \subseteq N_o$ is a set of credentials required to get access, $atLocation \in N$ s.t. $(n, atLocation) \in E$ is a model element from which access to n is granted (e.g. access from the office to the locker is granted with the key in the example in Sect. 2), and $EM \in N$ is a reference to the mechanism enabled in the model to enforce the policy. EM can be the same as $atLocation$, meaning that the enforcement mechanism is implemented right at the spot (e.g., a lock), it can be an actor (e.g., a security guard checking identity documents or a process implementing access control), or an object. Notice that we assume that $c \in Cred \subseteq N_o$ is an asset present in the model, which can be either an item or data.

In theory, different access control configurations of the same local policy δ_n can be enforced by different enforcement mechanisms. For example, to access a building employees might use a badge applying it to an RFID-reader, or they might show their IDs to a security guard.

3.2   AD-Bundles Generation

We will now show how to generate attack-defence bundles (AD-bundles) that can be used to capture the attack-defence state of the system. AD-bundles are generated for individual assets. They consist of attack nodes that correspond to gaining access to items in the model and attacking these items, and defence nodes that represent protections offered by the local policies in place. Notice that the bundles are attacker-agnostic, and they refer only to the system configuration regarding some particular item. Our notation abuses the standard notation for attack-defence trees, as we use AD-terms to represent both the tree structure and to refer to concrete attacker goals. We also define different types of AD-terms. This is syntactic sugar to ease the type representation, as types are used to put bundles together and synthesise AD-trees.

Attack node types. We consider attack nodes can be of the following types.

– $access_n$ is an attack node that represents that the attacker gains access to item n.

- $access\_from_{n,l}$ represents the goal of the attacker to access item n from specific model element l. This node type explicitly states the way n is accessed in the model, thus allowing us to understand immediately what access control policy is applicable (by looking at the $atLocation$ attribute).
- $break_n$ represents the goal of the attacker to somehow disable an access control mechanism implemented in n (this enforcement mechanism can protect assets not located in n).
- $attack\_pol_p$ represents the goal of the attacker to overcome protection of an individual access control configuration p.
- sat_pol_p represents attacker's goal to satisfy access control configuration p (by collecting all necessary credentials).

Defence node types. The defence nodes can be of the following types:

- $EM_{n,l}$ represents the defence of enforcement mechanisms enforcing policies at l to control access to n (notice that the enforcement mechanism itself can be located elsewhere).
- pol_config_p represents protection offered by an individual access control configuration for some $p \in \delta_n$.

Notice that term types $attack\_pol$ and pol_config are required to satisfy the requirement of AD trees for the unique child of the opposite type [11].

Bundle construction. Let $n \in N$ be an item in the model. An AD-bundle $\mathcal{B}_n$ that characterises accessing n is constructed as follows.

We start by setting the root of the bundle to $access_n$, as this is the desired attacker's goal.

Next, $access_n$ is refined:

$access_n := \vee^p \left(access\_from_{n,l} | l \in \mathtt{loc}(n) \right)$ // *n can be accessed only from an adjacent element in the model. Any of these elements is suitable for the attacker*

If $\nexists p = \langle Cred, l, EM \rangle \in \delta_n$ then
$access\_from_{n,l} := access_l$ // *access to n from l can be implemented by simply accessing l. No access control policy is set up to guard this connection.*

If $\exists p = \langle Cred, l, EM \rangle \in \delta_n$ then
$access\_from_{n,l} := c^p \left(access_l, EM_{n,l} \right)$ // *access to n from l can be implemented by accessing l. However, as there is an enforcement mechanism that controls access, the defence node is also added.*

$EM_{n,l} := \wedge^o \left(pol\_config_p | \forall p \in \delta_n \text{ s.t. } p = \langle Cred, l, s \rangle \right)$ // *Protection of access from l to n is implemented via individual policy configurations.*

$pol\_config_p := c^p \left(attack\_pol_p \right)$ // *syntactic sugar to switch back to attacker's view*

$attack\_pol_p := \vee^p \Big(sat\_pol_p, break_s \Big)$, where $p = \langle Cred, l, s \rangle$ // *Attacker can either satisfy the individual policy configuration p, or he can break the enforcement mechanism s that enforces this configuration p.*

$sat\_pol_p := \wedge^p \Big(access_{cred} | \forall cred \in Cred \Big)$, where $p = \langle Cred, l, s \rangle$ // *To satisfy the configuration the attacker needs to access all credentials in the set Cred identified in this configuration.*

We provide an example of an AD bundle in Fig. 1. By construction, for each bundle $\mathcal{B}_n$ its leaf nodes are either terms of the same type ($access_l$ for some l), or terms $break_s$. We do not refine terms of the type $break_s$ because the model itself lacks the knowledge how enforcement mechanisms can be broken. If an additional knowledge on breaking enforcement mechanisms will be available (e.g., as a hierarchy of attacks [17]), this term can further expanded.

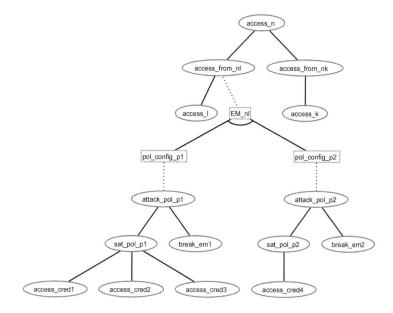

Fig. 1. An AD bundle.

3.3   Approach to Synthesise AD-Trees

AD-bundles represent attacks on individual assets in the model. They can be "glued" together to form AD-trees, in the spirit of attack generation by policy invalidation. In this subsection we outline an approach to synthesis of attack-defence trees.

The main requirement for AD-trees synthesis is that it should terminate. Indeed, it is easy to see that any simple loop in the infrastructure will create infinite trees if bundles are composed naively. Moreover, some bundles may appear more than once in the generated tree, creating duplicate subtrees. To avoid this, we introduce a system state that will keep track of already achieved progress and will allow to terminate the synthesis process when the attacker has achieved the goal.

State. We define now two functions that identify the state of the system. These functions will be updated as the attack tree is generated in order to keep track with the attack development.

Definition 1 (Reachable(,)). *Let* $\mathcal{M} = (N, E)$ *be a model. We define a boolean function* $\text{Reachable}(,) \subseteq N_a \times N$:

- *If* $(a, n) \in E$, $\text{Reachable}(a,n) := \text{True}$.
- *If for some* $l \in N_i$ $(a, l) \in E_{ai}$ *and* $(o, l) \in E_{oi}$, *then* $\text{Reachable}(a,o) := \text{True}$.
- *If for some* $l \in N_i$ $(a, l) \in E_{ai}$ *and* $(a_1, l) \in E_{ai}$, *then* $\text{Reachable}(a, a_1) := \text{True}$ *and* $\text{Reachable}(a_1, a) := \text{True}$.
- *Else* $\text{Reachable}(a, n) := \text{False}$

This function initially captures for a given actor all items immediately reachable in the model. These items can be objects or actors located in the same location as the actor. Let $\text{Reach}(a) := \{\forall n \in N \text{ s.t. } \text{Reachable}(a,n) = \text{True}\}$.

Definition 2 (Granted(,)). *We define a boolean function* $\text{Granted}(,) \subseteq N_a \times N$:

- *If for an item* n $\delta_n = \emptyset$ *then* $\text{Granted}(a,n) := \text{True}$.
- *If for an item* n *there is a tuple* $p = \langle Cred, atLocation \rangle \in \delta_n =$ *s.t.* $Cred \subseteq \text{Reach}(a) \cap N_o$ *then* $\text{Granted}(a,n) := \text{True}$.
- *Else* $\text{Granted}(a,n) := \text{False}$.

Intuitively, this function refers to some policy configuration that grants access to n. If $\text{Granted}(a,n) = \text{True}$, then there is a way for this actor to satisfy the access control policy for n (possibly under condition that he arrives at the right location).

Let us define a model state.

Definition 3 (State). *A generated state for a model* $\mathcal{M}$ *is a tuple* $\langle \text{Reachable}(,), \text{Granted}(,) \rangle$.

Definition 4 (Accessible(,)). *We define a boolean function* $\text{Accessible}(,) \subseteq N_a \times N$:

- $\text{Accessible}(a,n) := \text{Reachable}(a,n) \wedge \text{Granted}(a,n)$

Bootstrapping. Given a model $\mathcal{M} = \langle N, E \rangle$ produced by a modeller, the functions $\text{Reachable}(,)$, $\text{Granted}(,)$ and $\text{Accessible}(,)$ are initially computed from $\mathcal{M}$. First we compute a transitive closure of reachable locations:

- $\text{Reachable}(a,n) := \text{Reachable}(a,n) \vee (\exists l \in N : \text{Accessible}(a,l) \wedge ((l, n) \in E \vee (n, l) \in E))$

Notice that here we do not re-compute the function Granted(,), and thus, eventually, the reachable objects set for each actor will increase only with locations that are not guarded by access control policy. Once Reachable(,) is recomputed, it can be used to quickly evaluate whether an actor can reach certain locations in the original model (where may he end up).

Synthesis of AD-trees from Bundles. We now discuss composition of generated attack-defence trees. An attack-defence tree $\text{ADT}(\eta, \alpha)$ is synthesised for a chosen attacker $\eta \in N_a$ and a target asset $\alpha \in N_o$. The root node is the bundle $access_\alpha$. For each leaf node of the type $access_b$ we can compute its value by referring to the corresponding AD bundle $\mathcal{B}_b$.

Bundle Value. In the simplest case we use propositional semantics for evaluating AD-bundles and, eventually, AD-trees [11]. For leaf nodes of the type $access_n$, $access_n \equiv \text{Accessible}(\eta, n)$. For leaf nodes of the type $break_s$, $break_s \equiv \text{False}$ in the current synthesis approach. Thus, given a bundle for asset n, we can evaluate its value based on the values of the leaf nodes available. By updating the model state as attack progresses (more items become reachable to the attacker) we can eventually evaluate the target bundle, once all its descendants become evaluated. As state changes monotonically, the process will eventually terminate.

4   Introducing New Defences

The enforcement mechanisms for access control policies are not the only type of security controls that organisations use. Moreover, access control is not the only remedy that can be advised to improve security. Indeed, the existing risk analysis standards and security catalogues that guide practitioners in risk analysis identify many types of security controls and countermeasures. Many of those (for example, security cameras) cannot be captured by socio-technical models directly, because it will introduce unnecessary complications to the model. Some countermeasures can be introduced as properties of system elements (e.g., after a security training the employees might become less susceptible to social-engineering), but not as independent elements of the system.

We want to be able to update the attack-defence model of our system, captured by the suite of attack-defence bundles, after the first stage of automated generation. At this second stage we would like to obtain more complete attack-defence bundles with new defence nodes added that can capture additional security countermeasures (either existing in the model already or newly proposed once). We have two main questions associated with the newly introduced defences: *how to generate/propose new defences* and *where to place them in the attack-defence model* to keep the consistency across many attack scenarios and system updates. We start by addressing the second question first.

Where to Put New Countermeasures. Given an AD bundle representing the goal of an attacker to access asset n, two types of attack nodes are the candidates to be protected from by some countermeasures: the root node $access_n$ and its children $access\_from_{n,l}$. Indeed, for the connectors to other bundles (the leaf nodes $access_b$) it will make sense to introduce defences at the corresponding bundle to ensure the consistency requirement. For the nodes sat_pol_p, the attacker's goal is to satisfy the policy by finding the right credentials. It is not obvious what can be done as a protective measure besides protecting the credentials themselves. As for the nodes representing circumventing the enforcement mechanism, $break_s$, we do not have enough details for the moment how the attacker is going to break it. If this node is to be refined using some attack pattern library, it is better to create a separate AD bundle for treating the scenarios and assign defences there.

Now we have candidate attack nodes to be assigned countermeasures. To select the countermeasures that could be assigned, we first review existing types of security controls. It is well-established in the security industry to classify controls as preventive, detective and corrective [1]:

- *Preventive* controls focus on preventing security incidents from occurring.
- *Detective* controls focus on detecting occurrences of security incidents.
- *Corrective* controls focus on aiding the organisation to recover from a security incident.

From the implementation perspective, it is traditional to divide controls into the following categories [1]:

- *Technical* controls that are implemented typically as software controls.
- *Management*, or administrative, controls that are implemented as procedures and guidelines.
- *Operational* controls that focus on ensuring security and dependability of operations. These controls include physical security controls (physical access control, fire and water damage protection, etc.) and some controls that are difficult to classify as fully technical or physical (e.g., protection of personal computers).

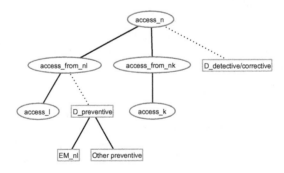

Fig. 2. An updated AD bundle with defence nodes in the designated positions (children of $EM_{(n,l)}$ not shown).

From this classification, we propose a way to update AD bundles with security controls in a consistent manner. The preventive controls can be added as children to the attack nodes $access\_from_{n,l}$, because they correspond to preventive measures for certain directed actions of the attacker. Access control policies present in the model are already embedded in the bundles at this position. To satisfy the attack-defence trees requirement of only one child of the opposite type, we will modify the bundle as in Fig. 2 (now the node $\mathcal{D}_{n,l}^{prev}$ is a parent of the node $EM_{n,l}$).

The detective and corrective measures can be added as children to the root node $access_n$ (see Fig. 2). In this position the defence nodes are directly linked to the system object in question, be it a location, a person, or an object. The semantics of the controls placed in this position are clear: assuming the attacker has already gained access to his target, is this detectable or what can be the remedy for this? Notice that some controls in practice can be both detective and preventive (e.g., security guards). In this case, it is safe to classify them as preventive controls.

What Defences to Choose. The choice of security controls is a tough question in practice. Not only it requires the human analyst to know possible attacks and countermeasures, but also the analyst needs to solve a complex multi-parameter optimisation problem. Indeed, the controls addressing the same threat can have different cost, efficiency and effectiveness. They can be more or less compliant with the industry standards and best practices. They can be more or less easy to implement and easy to verify. Finally, they can be more or less desired by the organisation because of personal views of the top-management. Thus, if we just consider the baseline controls listed by NIST Special Publication 800-53 [2], and try to evaluate all the above-mentioned parameters in order to fully automate the defence selection (now that we know where to place them), we already will face a very complex problem. Moreover, a single mistake in evaluation of some of the values will likely make the full analysis invalid. Therefore, it is likely that human-assisted control selection cannot be fully replaced by automated defence generation, at least for some time.

Yet, we can try to facilitate the defence selection problem by further categorising the security controls based on applicability to the scenarios in question and usefulness in attribute-based computations.

In the socio-technical model we have clear categories of objects: locations, actors and items that can belong to either physical or digital space. Thus controls can be chosen based already on simple considerations such as "access to digital objects by processes can be protected by using technical preventive controls", or "access of humans to humans can be protected by administrative and physical preventive controls". Table 1 summarises these choices of controls. In this table, it is expected that respective controls will be introduced in the dedicated AD bundles (following the template in Fig. 2).

Furthermore, following the investigation of attribute decoration on attack-defence trees by Bagnato et al. [4], we can look at what controls contribute to computations of certain attributes. For instance, if the analyst is interested

Table 1. Controls selection based on system elements.

Entity	Physical space	Digital space
Preventive		
Location	Physical access control	Technical access control, firewall
Actor	Physical access control, Security trainings, Email filter	Technical access control and authentication
Object	Physical access control	Technical access control
Detective		
Location	Security cameras, visitor logs	System logs, IDS
Actor		
Object		
Corrective		
Location	Insurance, liability limitation, business continuity plan	Insurance, liability limitation, secure state restoring mechanisms, business continuity plan
Actor		
Object		

in the probability of an attack to succeed, the minimal cost of attack for an attacker, or time of executing an attack, then (under the assumption that detection cannot stop the attack) she would like to look at her preventive measures. If she is interested in the impact the attack has on her organisation (how business continuity is affected after the attack was executed), she would like to consider the preventive and corrective controls, especially the latter ones, because these ensure business continuity. Thus, if she is interested only in some attributes, the computation on AD bundles does not need to take into account all controls at once. Table 2 summarises the control types that are the most relevant for some selected attributes.

Table 2. Relevant controls for example attributes

Attribute	Preventive	Detective	Corrective
Risk of detection		✓	
Cost of attack (for attacker)	✓		
Probability of attack success	✓		
Time of attack	✓		
Impact of attack	✓	✓	✓

Notice that the controls added at this stage will probably not follow the AD bundle notation, but will be expressed in the natural language (e.g., *security training* or *ID check*). This is understandable, because, as we have mentioned, models are not rich enough by nature. Yet, this is acceptable for the format, because the attack-defence model does not need to be fully formal. On the contrary, it is used to assist the human analyst to create and maintain the attack-defence view on the system. The only requirement that we have for it is the consistency, which is ensured by adding each control only to the bundle representing the attack-defence view of a particular (unique) entity in the model. Some controls can require a notion of *perimeter* to be defined in the model, so that they can be uniquely assigned to the bundle corresponding to the perimeter, and not to each entity belonging to that perimeter. This is easily implementable in any socio-technical model.

5 Related Work

The question of attack trees generation from system models has been tackled in [8]. Similarly, [14,22] worked on generating attack models from a system model. While we follow the same approach for attacker's view, our main focus is on keeping both attacker's and defender's views consistent with the main socio-technical model.

Attack-countermeasure trees (ACTs) is an alternative model to attack-defence trees in keeping both views simultaneously [20]. In [21] the authors have investigated optimal countermeasure selection for ACTs when a set of possible countermeasures to be implemented is already predefined. It will be interesting to investigate ACTs suitability for the attack-defence model, because they support explicit detection and mitigation countermeasure nodes (but not corrective).

In [12] the authors work on directly applying model checking to a socio-technical model in order to evaluate some reachability-based security properties.

Ferreira et al. [6] have discussed defences suggestion in the context of the socio-technical model STEAL. They propose to apply defences at the technical and social levels of the system, what is in line with our proposal for applying security control categories in selecting defences.

6 Conclusion and the Next Steps

In this work we have approached the question of creating and maintaining the security controls representation in parallel to the socio-technical model. Our solution creates a set of attack-defence bundles (small attack-defence trees) that can be maintained with a socio-technical model as its separate view. The bundles are generated from the model in the beginning, but afterwards they are enriched consistently alongside the new security controls identified by a human analyst. We have also discussed how new controls can be selected based on the model entities and the attributes of interest to the analyst. This work attempts to bridge the gap between the approach of automated attack generation from system model and the manual security control selection in the traditional risk analysis. The next step is to look into the compositional attack-defence tree synthesis for more complex attribute domains. After that, it will be possible to investigate optimal countermeasure selection, based, e.g., on the approaches suggested in [3,21]. Another further research direction is practical validation of the proposed approach on realistic case studies and evaluation of its usefulness and scalability.

Acknowledgements. This work was partially supported by the European Commission through the FP7 project TREsPASS (grant agreement n. 318003) and by Fonds National de la Recherche Luxembourg through the ADT2P project (grant n. C13/IS/5809105).

References

1. NIST Special Publication 800–30 Guide for conducting risk assessments. revision 1 (2012). http://csrc.nist.gov/publications/nistpubs/800-30-rev1/sp800_30_r1.pdf
2. NIST Special Publication 800–53 Revision 4. Security and privacy controls for federal information systems and organizations (2013). http://nvlpubs.nist.gov/nistpubs/SpecialPublications/NIST.SP.800-53r4.pdf
3. Aslanyan, Z., Nielson, F.: Pareto efficient solutions of attack-defence trees. In: Focardi, R., Myers, A. (eds.) POST 2015. LNCS, vol. 9036, pp. 95–114. Springer, Heidelberg (2015)
4. Bagnato, A., Kordy, B., Meland, P.H., Sweitzer, P.: Attribute decoration of attack-defence trees. IJSSE **3**(2), 1–35 (2012)
5. Dimkov, T., Pieters, W., Hartel, P.: Portunes: representing attack scenarios spanning through the physical, digital and social domain. In: Armando, A., Lowe, G. (eds.) ARSPA-WITS 2010. LNCS, vol. 6186, pp. 112–129. Springer, Heidelberg (2010)
6. Ferreira, A., Huynen, J.-L., Koenig, V., Lenzini, G.: A conceptual framework to study socio-technical security. In: Tryfonas, T., Askoxylakis, I. (eds.) HAS 2014. LNCS, vol. 8533, pp. 318–329. Springer, Heidelberg (2014)
7. Ford, M., Rensink, A., Willemson, J., Lenin, A., Probst, C.W., Gadyatskaya, O., Trujillo-Rasua, R., Hansen, R.R., Othman, B.: TREsPASS D3.4.1 Attack generation from socio-technical models (2014)
8. Ivanova, M.G., Probst, C.W., Hansen, R.R., Kammuller, F.: Transforming graphical system models to graphical attack models. In: Mauw, S., et al. (eds.) GraMSec 2015. LNCS, vol. 9390, pp. 82–96. Springer, Heidelberg (2016)
9. Kammuller, F., Probst, C.W.: Invalidating policies using structural information. In: Proceedings of IEEE S & P Workshops, pp. 229–235. IEEE (2013)
10. Kordy, B., Ivanova, M.G., Hansen, R.R., Probst, C.: TREsPASS D1.3.1 Initial prototype of socio-technical security model (2013)
11. Kordy, B., Mauw, S., Radomirovic, S., Schweitzer, P.: Attack-defense trees. J. Logic Comput. **24**(1), 55–87 (2014). Oxford University Press
12. Lenzini, G., Mauw, S., Ouchani, S.: Security analysis of socio-technical physical systems. Elsevier Comput. Electr. Eng. (2015)
13. Othmane, L., Ranchal, R., Fernando, R., Bhargava, B.K., Bodden, E.: Incorporating attacker capabilities in risk estimation and mitigation. Elsevier Comput. Secur. **51**, 41–61 (2015)

14. Ou, X., Boyer, W., McQueen, M.: A scalable approach to attack graph generation. In: Proceedings of CCS, pp. 336–345. ACM (2006)
15. Paul, S.: Technique for automating the construction and maintenance of attack trees. In: Proceedings of GraMSec, vol. 148, pp. 31–46. EPTCS (2014)
16. Pieters, W.: Representing humans in system security models: an actor-network approach. J. Wirel. Mob. Netw. Ubiquit. Comput. Dependable Appl. 2(1), 75–92 (2012)
17. Pinchinat, S., Acher, M., Vojtisek, D.: Towards synthesis of attack trees for supporting computer-aided risk analysis. In: Canal, C., Idani, A. (eds.) SEFM 2014 Workshops. LNCS, vol. 8938, pp. 363–375. Springer, Heidelberg (2015)
18. Probst, C.W., Hansen, R.R.: An extensible analysable system model. Inf. Secur. Tech. Rep. 13(4), 235–246 (2008)
19. Radomirovic, S., Basin, D., Schlapfer, M.: A complete characterization of secure human-server communication. In: Proceedings of CSF. IEEE (2015)
20. Roy, A., Kim, D., Trivedi, K.: ACT: towards unifying the constructs of attack and defense trees. Secur. Commun. Netw. 3, 1–15 (2011)
21. Roy, A., Kim, D., Trivedi, K.: Scalable optimal countermeasure selection using implicit enumeration on attack countermeasure trees, pp. 1–12 (2012)
22. Vigo, R., Nielsen, F., Nielson, H.R.: Automated generation of attack trees. In: Proceedings of CSF, pp. 337–350. IEEE (2014)

Guided Specification and Analysis of a Loyalty Card System

Laurent Cuennet[1], Marc Pouly[2]([✉]), and Saša Radomirović[3]

[1] Department of Informatics, University of Fribourg, Fribourg, Switzerland
[2] Lucerne University of Applied Sciences and Arts, Lucerne, Switzerland
marc.pouly@hslu.ch
[3] Department of Computer Science, Institute of Information Security,
ETH Zürich, Zürich, Switzerland

Abstract. We apply a graphical model to develop a digital loyalty program protocol specifically tailored to small shops with no professional or third-party-provided infrastructure. The graphical model allows us to capture assumptions on the environment the protocol is running in, such as capabilities of agents, available channels and their security properties. Moreover, the model serves as a manual tool to quickly rule out insecure protocol designs and to focus on improving promising designs. We illustrate this by a step-wise improvement of a crude but commercially used protocol to finally derive a light-weight and scalable security protocol with proved security properties and many appealing features for practical use.

1 Introduction

Paper-based ink stamp cards are a convenient and inexpensive way for small shops to improve customer loyalty. Other than an ink stamp and printed cards, no further materials nor infrastructure are required. And unlike common customer loyalty programs of large enterprises [9], such cards guarantee customer privacy. The typical example for the application of paper-based loyalty cards is the independent coffee shop around the corner that offers a free drink for every 10 stamps collected. Customers using these cards cannot be tracked and profiled, and they can easily transfer their cards to someone else.

A common problem for loyalty points hunters is the number of stamp cards that accumulate over time. With mobile devices being widely available, the straightforward idea is to implement the functionality of paper-based loyalty cards as a mobile app. With special focus on small shops, such a system must first and foremost be light-weight. The cost of an electronic loyalty points solution should not be orders of magnitude larger than the paper-based system. This precludes solutions that are based on third-party-provided infrastructure or professional check-out systems known from large retailers. A likely solution scenario is that a vendor provides loyalty points with QR codes that are scanned by the customers' mobile devices.

S. Mauw et al. (Eds.): GraMSec 2015, LNCS 9390, pp. 66–81, 2016.
DOI: 10.1007/978-3-319-29968-6_5

In this paper, we consider the problem of designing a secure loyalty points protocol along the restrictions sketched above. This problem serves as a case study for the applicability of *communication topologies*, a graphical approach to modeling security assumptions, to guide the design of secure protocols.

The protocols we design are simple and the steps we have taken seem self-evident in retrospect. On the one hand, the imposed infrastructural constraints naturally enforce simplicity, on the other hand, this makes loyalty points protocols a perfect case study for a detailed walk-through with our design methodology. In this spirit, we encourage the reader to pause the reading of the paper at the end of Sect. 2.1 and to design a secure loyalty points protocol satisfying the requirements stated in that section. The reader can then analyze his or her protocol with the same methods that we apply to our first protocol in Sect. 3.

We have formally verified two of the protocols we design in this paper and we give a brief account of the results in Sect. 4. To complete our story, we discuss implementation aspects of a practical loyalty card system in Sect. 5. We discuss related work in Sect. 6 and conclude in Sect. 7.

2   Preliminaries

We briefly state the security requirements that an electronic loyalty points protocol should satisfy. Then we introduce the communication topology, a model on which our methodology for secure protocol design is based. The definitions given in this section are purposefully informal.

2.1   Security Requirements

A classical loyalty points system consists of a vendor that issues loyalty points to a customer commensurate with the customer's purchase. In the point-per-product-purchased loyalty card system frequently used by coffee shops the vendor issues a loyalty point by stamping a mark on a paper card for every coffee purchased. One mark is equivalent to one loyalty point, and the customer may redeem a certain number of loyalty points for a free coffee.

In the electronic loyalty points system we replace the stamp by the shop's computer or mobile device, to which we will refer as *server*, and the paper card by the customer's mobile device. The loyalty points are digital information. Thus, the electronic system consists of four agents: The customer, the vendor, the mobile device of the customer, and the shop's server.

An electronic loyalty points system should ideally satisfy all the security requirements that a paper-based system satisfies, among which we consider the following as important:

Unforgeability of points: Every loyalty point accepted by the vendor has been issued by the vendor.
No double-spending of points: A loyalty point that was previously redeemed will not be accepted by the vendor.

Customer anonymity: The vendor cannot link points issued to or redeemed by a customer to the customer's identity.

Customer privacy: The vendor cannot link a returning customer's transaction to the customer's previous transactions.

Theft protection of points: Points issued to an agent can be redeemed by this agent.

Non-repudiation by vendor: The vendor cannot repudiate the validity of an unredeemed loyalty point issued to a customer.

A paper-based loyalty points system satisfies the unforgeability, no double-spending and non-repudiation requirements, but it typically does not satisfy the theft-protection requirement, since a loyalty card can be stolen. Sometimes, when plain ink stamps from a retailer are being used, unforgeability of points requires the vendor to additionally sign each point manually. Customer anonymity is also guaranteed, unless the vendor knows the customer personally, but customer privacy may only hold to a certain degree. If the vendor provides each loyalty card with additional information, some limited profiling becomes possible. The vendor may for example use a date stamp in order to profile coffee consumption of anonymous individuals and must additionally provide each loyalty card with a unique serial number, if the information from different loyalty cards is to be linked to the same anonymous individual.

As with paper-based loyalty points systems, it can be argued that an electronic system may not satisfy the theft-protection requirement if the customer's mobile device is stolen. However, in the following we assume that the agent receiving loyalty points is the mobile device. In other words, we are not protecting against theft of the mobile device, but against the case where points issued to a customer's mobile device cannot be redeemed by that device. We note that there are two ways in which the theft-protection requirement could fail: (1) Points issued to a mobile device are redeemed by an attacker's device and (2) points issued to a mobile device are corrupted or lost and thus not redeemable by the device. We therefore refine theft-protection into two classical security requirements: a confidentiality requirement to prevent scenario (1) and authenticity of loyalty points issued by the vendor to prevent scenario (2). A term x (e.g., a loyalty point or cryptographic key) is said to be *confidential* (or secret), if the attacker does not know it. A term x received in a communication apparently from Y is said to be *authentic*, if Y indeed sent x. We will focus on these two requirements in the remainder of the paper. These requirements are formalized in our models of two loyalty points protocols discussed in Sect. 4.

2.2 Communication Topologies

A communication topology is a graph-theoretic model of communication protocol assumptions [3]. It contains assumptions on role capabilities, initial knowledge of roles, channel availability, and security assumptions on channels. A communication topology thus represents a set of protocols: All protocols that satisfy the stated assumptions. Given a communication topology τ, we may ask whether any of the protocols that satisfy the assumptions of τ also satisfy a given security requirement, e.g., one or more of the requirements stated in the preceding section.

Formally, a communication topology is an edge- and vertex-labeled directed graph (V, E, η, μ), where V is a set of role names, $E \subseteq V \times V$ and η and μ are functions assigning labels to vertices and edges respectively. For $A, B \in V$, an edge $(A, B) \in E$ denotes the availability of a communication channel from the agent executing role A to the agent executing role B. We call a sequence of vertices $[v_1, \ldots, v_{k+1}]$ with $v_1, \ldots, v_{k+1} \in V$ such that $(v_i, v_{i+1}) \in E$ for $1 \le i \le k$ a *path* from v_1 to v_{k+1}.

The vertex labeling function η assigns capability, knowledge, and trust assumptions to role names, i.e., to the vertices in the graph. The edge labeling function μ assigns security assumptions to communication channels. The communication channels defined in [3] are denoted by $\circ\!\!-\!\!\circ, \bullet\!\!-\!\!\circ, \circ\!\!-\!\!\bullet, \bullet\!\!-\!\!\bullet$ and represent, respectively, the insecure, authentic, confidential, and secure communication channel. An insecure channel is defined as a channel that the attacker can eavesdrop on, modify messages transmitted on it, and inject arbitrary messages into it. An authentic channel prevents modification of messages. More precisely, it guarantees to the recipient of a message that the message was previously sent by the sender. The attacker can still eavesdrop on an authentic channel. The confidential channel prevents the attacker from eavesdropping on messages, but allows the attacker to inject his own messages. The secure channel is defined to be an authentic and confidential channel. That is, the attacker can neither eavesdrop on nor modify messages.

Figure 1 shows the communication topology that we refer to as the *coffee shop topology* and work with in the remainder of this paper. It contains four nodes: the customer C, the vendor V, the customer's mobile device D, and the vendor's server S. All four nodes are assumed to be honest and initially share no private information. Customer and vendor are *human* roles, which is indicated by a dashed circle. Their capabilities are restricted in that they cannot perform any

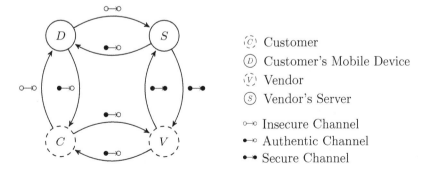

Fig. 1. The coffee shop topology.

computations beyond concatenating and splitting messages. The mobile device and server have no such restrictions, as indicated by a solid circle.

The channel assumptions in the coffee shop topology are as follows. The communication channels between customer C and vendor V are authentic. This is justified by the fact that the customer and vendor are physically facing each other and thus able to attribute messages that they hear or paper notes that they receive to the correct source, e.g., the person in front of them. The channel from the mobile device D to the customer is assumed to be authentic, based on the assumption that the customer recognizes his own device. We assume that the channel from the customer to the device is insecure, because the customer might not be using an authentication mechanism on his device and might not always keep the device in his own possession. The channel from the device to the shop's server S is insecure, since any device could be messaging the server or eavesdrop on a communication. In particular, we assume that the server does not share any longterm secret keys with the device D, as this might clash with the privacy requirement. The channel from server to mobile device is assumed to be authentic, since the server's public key can be authentically distributed in the shop. It could be posted as a QR code on a wall that is only accessible by the vendor. However, if the reader is concerned about an unnoticeable replacement of the QR code by an attacker, we can always instruct the shop assistant to carry a shirt with an imprinted QR code. Finally, the communication channels between the server and the vendor are assumed to be secure, since this can be physically ensured.

Communication topologies can be given a semantics [3] that is aligned with the semantics of the Tamarin prover tool [13]. We have used the Tamarin prover tool to verify two of our protocols as discussed in Sect. 4.

3   Designing a Simple Loyalty Card Protocol

We start with a naive protocol and improve it in two steps with the help of the coffee shop topology into a protocol that satisfies the security requirements stated in Sect. 2.1. As we aim to design a scalable loyalty card system, see Sect. 5, we subsequently focus on the more comprehensive *point-per-euro-spent system* that incorporates the lighter variant of a *point-per-product-purchased system* from our coffee shop example, and which can also be used for retailers with a wider variety of goods.

3.1   First Protocol

Consider a first electronic loyalty card protocol to issue loyalty points to a customer, shown in Fig. 2. The protocol runs as follows. The customer pays the vendor a certain amount of money for a purchase. The vendor then enters the amount of money paid into the server S. The server returns a number of points that depends on the amount of money paid to the vendor (or the number of products sold). The separator / in message 3 of the protocol indicates that the

LP-1 1. $C \to V$:   money
LP-1 2. $V \to S$:   money
LP-1 3. $S \to V$:   points(money) / QRcode
LP-1 4. $V \to C$:   QRcode
LP-1 5. $C \to D$:   QRcode / points(money)

Fig. 2. Protocol LP-1: A first protocol for issuing loyalty points

server sends a message that encodes *points(money)*, but that the vendor (due to his computational restriction) is unable to parse this message and verify its correctness. To the vendor, it is simply a QR code. The vendor gives the QR code to the customer. The customer then uses his mobile device to scan the code. The device can parse the scanned code and extract the number of points obtained.

By the assumptions in our coffee shop topology, the channel from the vendor to the customer is authentic, but not confidential and the channel from the customer to his mobile device is an insecure channel. It follows that there are two opportunities for an attacker to observe the QR code: When the customer receives it and when it is scanned by the device. This is a problem if the QR code must be kept secret. For instance, if the information represented by the QR code is sufficient to redeem the encoded loyalty point then the protocol LP-1 has no theft protection.

Remark. We have observed an even simpler system in use in Switzerland: One loyalty point is awarded by the vendor per product sold and the *same QR code* is used for every transaction. The QR code is printed on a piece of cardboard that the vendor shows to the customer. The mobile device's app essentially counts the number of times it has scanned the QR code. This system offers theft protection to everyone: Since all loyalty points are represented by the same digital information and are redeemable, nobody's points can be stolen. However, the system does not satisfy the double-spending requirement. Instead of scanning the QR code with the system's official mobile app, an attacker can take a photograph and redeem the same point over and over again. Due to the absence of a secure protocol, these merchants try to counteract such attacks with various infrastructural and legal measures.

Returning to protocol LP-1, our goal is to ensure the secrecy of the QR code in order to satisfy the theft protection requirement. We have two options to protect the secrecy of the QR code. The first option is to strengthen the assumptions made in the coffee shop topology. We must assume that (1) the channel from the vendor to the customer is a secure channel and (2) that the channel from the customer to his mobile device is confidential. The justification for (1) could be that the QR code is given to the customer in a concealed manner, e.g., on the counter-facing side of a paper. This assumption is not uncommon: Phone credit top-ups are in some countries sold as paper-printed codes. However, we have yet to see a vendor that takes precautionary steps to keep the printed code concealed. The justification for (2) is that the customer always scans the QR code in a private environment. We believe, however, that this is too inconvenient to be carried out in practice. The second and preferred option is to improve the protocol.

3.2 Second Protocol

The QR code of protocol LP-1 does not have to be secret if it is an encryption of the loyalty points or if the loyalty points that it encodes satisfy the theft-protection requirement by another mechanism. In both cases, the server must know information related to C or D to protect the loyalty points. We must therefore solve the following problem: How to send information authentically (or even securely) from D to S?

It is not possible to send information authentically (and hence neither securely) from D to S in the coffee shop topology using *only* the two edges (D, S) and (S, D) that directly connect D and S: The edge (D, S) is labeled as insecure and (S, D) as authentic, but in the wrong direction. This impossibility can be proved formally [3, Lemma 2].

It is, however, possible to send information authentically (but not confidentially) along the path $[D, C, V, S]$, because all edges along this path are labeled as authentic or secure and C and V are honest. We thus have an authentic channel from D to S along this path and an authentic channel from S to D by the edge (S, D).

LP-2 1.	$C \rightarrow D$:	GetPoints
LP-2 2.	$D \rightarrow C$:	PointsCode
LP-2 3.	$C \rightarrow V$:	money, PointsCode
LP-2 4.	$V \rightarrow S$:	money, PointsCode
LP-2 5.	$S \rightarrow V$:	$\{\text{points(money)}\}_{\text{PointsCode}}$ / QRcode
LP-2 6.	$V \rightarrow C$:	QRcode
LP-2 7.	$C \rightarrow D$:	QRcode / $\{\text{points(money)}\}_{\text{PointsCode}}$

Fig. 3. Protocol LP-2: Improved protocol for issuing loyalty points

We can therefore improve upon our first protocol as follows. The mobile device creates a *points code* (an ephemeral public key) that is sent authentically to the server. The server uses this code to encrypt the loyalty points. The protocol is shown in Fig. 3. We denote the encryption of a message m with the public key k by $\{m\}_k$. However, in spite of the encryption, the protocol does not protect against theft. We see this problem in the coffee shop topology: The channel from the customer to the device is insecure. An attacker can therefore replace the message from customer to device by a different message, e.g., by a redeemed loyalty point encrypted (by the attacker) under the device's points code. We must, however, admit that this scenario stretches the limits of our imagination.

We thus have again two options: Change the channel assumption or improve the protocol. We again choose the latter.

3.3   The Third Protocol: A Simple Loyalty Card Protocol

Protocol LP-2 fails to satisfy a security property because the path $[S, V, C, D]$ does not provide an authentic channel from S to D. (This is because the final edge of the path (C, D) is insecure.) There is still, however, the *direct* authentic channel from S to D and the protocol can be easily modified to take advantage of this channel, as shown in Fig. 4.

SLP 1.	$C \rightarrow D$:	GetPoints
SLP 2.	$D \rightarrow C$:	PointsCode
SLP 3.	$C \rightarrow V$:	money, PointsCode
SLP 4.	$V \rightarrow S$:	money, PointsCode
SLP 5.	$S \rightarrow D$:	$\{\text{points(money)}\}_{\text{PointsCode}}$

Fig. 4. Protocol SLP: Further improved protocol for issuing loyalty points

We have found a protocol that may plausibly satisfy the theft protection requirement. Furthermore, if the function that generates points based on the amount of the purchase is chosen appropriately, the protocol can satisfy the unforgeability requirement and, if the server keeps track of all points that were generated, the double-spending requirement can be satisfied. However, the privacy and non-repudiation requirements are not satisfied. For non-repudiation the vendor must commit to their validity by signing them for instance. In protocol SLP, no signatures are specified.

Message 5 in protocol SLP is assumed to be sent over an authentic channel from S to D. The security assumption on this channel is different from the other channel assumptions in that we have based it on a cryptographic assumption: "The channel is assumed to be authentic, because the server's public key can be authentically distributed in the shop." That is, to realize the authenticity property of this channel, the server must digitally sign message 5 and the device must verify the signature with the (authentic) public key that it has received. The signature on message 5 can be used towards the non-repudiation requirement. We note that in such a case a customer would have to rely on the legal system recognizing digital signatures as a non-repudiation mechanism. A likely precondition for this is that the public key is certified for such a use and the customer would need to verify the certificate. We consider this issue to be outside of the scope of the protocol specification and accept a server's signature that is verifiable with the authentically distributed public key to be a sufficient non-repudiation token.

The protocol does not satisfy the privacy requirement, because the vendor can link the issued points when they are collectively redeemed to the shopping baskets and points in time that they were issued.

3.4   An Ecash-Based Loyalty Card Protocol

We now present our final improvement on the series of protocols. To provide customer privacy, we import a solution from the digital cash domain, which is a protocol based on blind signatures. In the loyalty card version of the digital cash protocol, the roles of the mint, bank, and merchant are combined in the shop's server. To keep the customer's different transactions unlinkable, the device chooses the serial numbers of coins and the server issues a blind signature on it. To prevent cheating, the device and server need to run a cut-and-choose protocol. Such protocols are standard (we discuss a specific example in Sect. 5) and we can consider them a simple building block. What we therefore need to ensure is that the server and device can establish a secure channel in the coffee shop topology. The secure key establishment phase is shown in Fig. 5. The protocol runs as follows. When the mobile device receives the GetPoints instruction from the customer, it generates an ephemeral private key (eskD) and displays the corresponding public key, pk(eskD), to the customer. The customer pays the vendor and shows the mobile device's display to the vendor. The vendor inputs the transaction amount into the server and scans the code displayed on the customer's mobile device with the server. The server has thus received the device's public key. The server generates a session key SessKey, encrypts it with the device's public key, signs it with its own private key, and transmits the message to the device. This transmission could be done via NFC, Bluetooth, or WiFi. The server and device can now run any protocol over the secure channel that they have just established. At the end of this protocol the device displays to the customer the number of points received.

PP 1.	$C \rightarrow D$:	GetPoints
PP 2.	$D \rightarrow C$:	pk(eskD) / code
PP 3.	$C \rightarrow V$:	money, code
PP 4.	$V \rightarrow S$:	money, code / money, pk(eskD)
PP 5.	$S \rightarrow D$:	sign($\{\text{SessKey}\}_{\text{pk(eskD)}}, sk(S)$)
PP :.	$D \rightarrow S$:	...
PP :.	$S \rightarrow D$:	...
PP n.	$D \rightarrow C$:	number of points received

Fig. 5. Protocol PP: key setup for PrivatePoints

4   Security Analysis

We have verified [17] authenticity and secrecy of the session key 'SessKey' of the PP protocol with the Tamarin tool [13]. The verification considers an unbounded number of sessions and assumes that there are compromised agents in the system.

Since the session key is used to provide a secure channel between the server and the device, the remaining security requirements for the PrivatePoints system follow from the security properties of the ecash sub-protocol.

The protocol that was verified is given in Fig. 6, which makes explicit what initial knowledge assumptions are made and which terms are assumed to be randomly generated. The former is denoted by the "knows" keyword and the latter by the "fresh" keyword in the figure.

C knows: D, V
D knows: $C, S, \mathrm{pk}(S)$
V knows: S
S knows: $V, \mathrm{sk}(S)$
PP 1. $C \to D$:   GetPoints
PP 2. $D \to C$:   fresh(eskD). pk(eskD) / code
PP 3. $C \to V$:   money, code
PP 4. $V \to S$:   money, code / money, pk(eskD)
PP 5. $S \to D$:   fresh(SessKey). sign($\{$SessKey$\}_{\mathrm{pk(eskD)}}, \mathrm{sk}(S)$)

Fig. 6. Protocol PP: Specification for the SessionKey exchange for PrivatePoints

Note that the same analysis shows that our simple loyalty points protocol SLP (Sect. 3.3) satisfies secrecy and authenticity of loyalty points. In SLP, the randomly generated number is not used as a session key, but rather as an identifier for the issued loyalty points. The protocol to *redeem points* in the simple loyalty points system is nearly identical to the protocol PP in Fig. 6. The main difference is an additional sixth message in which the points to be redeemed are communicated from the device to the server. Its specification is shown in Fig. 7. For this protocol, we have verified [17] the secrecy and authenticity of the points transmitted from the device to the server.

C knows: D, V
D knows: $C, S, \mathrm{pk}(S), points$
V knows: S
S knows: $V, \mathrm{sk}(S), points$
rSLP 1. $C \to D$:   SpendPoints
rSLP 2. $D \to C$:   fresh(eskD). pk(eskD) / code
rSLP 3. $C \to V$:   redeem, code
rSLP 4. $V \to S$:   redeem, code / redeem, pk(eskD)
rSLP 5. $S \to D$:   fresh(SessKey). sign($\{$SessKey$\}_{\mathrm{pk(eskD)}}, \mathrm{sk}(S)$)
rSLP 6. $D \to S$: $\{$points$\}_{\mathrm{SessKey}}$

Fig. 7. Protocol rSLP: Specification for redeeming loyalty points.

5   Towards a Practical Loyalty Points System

Design and formal verification of a security protocol is one part of the story; equally important, though, are aspects and protocol features that directly impact implementation in a real-world setting. We therefore discuss our experience in implementing a prototype of a loyalty points system that we call *Private Points* [8].

5.1   Private Points

We first discuss briefly how a particular digital cash solution has been used to issue and redeem points and afterwards report on implementation aspects.

Issuing Loyalty Points. The sub-protocol to issue loyalty points we have chosen follows essentially the ecash protocol of Schoenmakers [19], with a few simplifying changes.

1. The server communicates to the device how many points will be issued.
2. For every coin C_i to be generated by the server, the device generates a secret serial number x_i.
3. The serial numbers are hashed, blinded, and transmitted to be blindly signed by the server.
4. The device verifies the signatures for all coins received.

Redeeming Loyalty Points. As the PrivatePoints system is limited to the roles of customer, vendor, mobile device, and server, it is the server that needs to play the role of the bank (see the original ecash protocol [19] for the role specification). Most importantly, the server needs to check the validity of loyalty points and prevent double spending, as well as guarantee non-repudiation to the user as discussed above. The following is a high-level view of the protocol.

1. The customer selects a number of loyalty points to redeem for an item.
2. All the selected points C_i are transmitted by the mobile device to the server, each with the hash of the secret serial number $h(x_i)$ in order for the server to verify the loyalty point signature.
3. The server verifies the points received by checking the signature and verifying that the points have not been previously spent.
   Note that if the shop maliciously claimed that a valid coin has been spent already, the user could ask for the coin number as proof of the claim. Since the shop is only in possession of the *hashed* coin number at this point of the payment process, it is unable to uphold the claim.
4. The server sends a signature to the device confirming that the received points are valid for this transaction. This step is crucial for the non-repudiation requirement.
5. The device verifies the server's signature. If the signature is valid, the device sends the secret serial numbers x_i.
6. The server verifies that the serial numbers produce the previously received hashes.

5.2   Implementation

While a small coffee shop could perhaps afford to invest in a reasonably priced loyalty points infrastructure, an ice cream vendor in a football stadium carrying an ice box definitely can not. Consequently, the only infrastructure we can assume for customers and shops are plain mobile devices exchanging loyalty points over a near-field communication link, for example. PrivatePoints has been designed especially with this scenario in mind. The protocol does not require any online registration prior to its first use as this would spoil the security measures taken to ensure customer anonymity.

Moreover, PrivatePoints is efficient enough to be used in the train station's coffee shop during rush hour and allows for collecting multiple points in one go in case people treat each other to coffee, or if the point-per-euro-spent system is implemented. As a rule of thumb, our industry partners give a limit of $2\,$s that can be invested on issuing loyalty points during the payment process. With transmission and protocol overhead subtracted, cryptographic operations must therefore not take more than $800\,$ms on off-the-shelf mobile phones. In case of PrivatePoints, issuing digital loyalty points consists of hashing a serial number and providing and verifying a blinded signature. Our implementation on a SAMSUNG GT-I9100 mobile phone with the Android operating system using SHA-256 and RSA-2048 produces one coin every $40\,$ms on average, thus 20 coins in $800\,$ms.

Finally, Loyalty card systems should not require an Internet connection. This is because small shops may be located in places with poor Internet connectivity or provide only a slow connection. During rush hour it is unacceptable to invest several seconds per customer to set up Internet connection for the loyalty points exchange. From a business point of view, this is probably the most important feature of the PrivatePoints protocol which is not related to security.

6   Related Work

There are a variety of approaches to guided protocol design and we briefly highlight a few of them. Abadi and Needham give principles for the design of secure cryptographic protocols [1]. These principles are not intended to be sufficient or necessary for secure protocols, but constitute prudent engineering practice that prevents common confusions and mistakes. The AGVI toolkit [20] provides automatic protocol generation and implementation tools. The designer inputs a system specification and security requirements into the protocol generator that produces candidate protocols. The candidate protocols are analyzed by a model checker and verified protocols are translated to Java by a code generator. A similar approach is taken in the GSD framework [15,16], where the protocol designer inputs an abstract protocol specification and security requirements into a tool that acts as an interface to different protocol verification tools. Sprenger and Basin [22] propose a development method for security protocols based on stepwise refinement. The designer starts with an abstract security goal and successively refines the goal into a secure cryptographic protocol. Each refinement step is developed together with a correctness proof and thus the resulting protocol satisfies the specified security goal by construction.

In contrast to the above approaches, we explicitly consider human agents in the communication protocol. We use the communication topologies model to specify and graphically represent the given security assumptions in the system and then use the graphical representation to guide the specification of a security protocol.

Communication topologies have been introduced in the context of secure human-server communication [3]. They were used to classify all four-node topologies that consist of a human, a device, a corrupted computing platform belonging to the human, and a remote server. The classification distinguishes between topologies that have secure communication protocols and those for which provably no such protocols exist. The communication topologies' channel notation o—o, •—o, o—•, •—• was introduced by Maurer and Schmid [12] and used to define transformation rules for secure channel establishment with cryptographic primitives.

Ecash was invented and subsequently commercialized by David Chaum [6]. Since about the mid-1990's, the topic of digital cash payment systems, their properties, and technical foundations is extensively covered in the literature, e.g., [2,14,18,19,21,23]. One might argue that loyalty points are merely a particular type of non-universal, virtual currency. However, there is a fundamental difference between loyalty systems and virtual currencies. A currency is issued by a bank or mint that acts as a trusted third party in protocols between customers and vendors. In case of a loyalty points system, bank and vendor conglomerate to a single party, which breaks the trust relation between customer and bank. PrivatePoints is to a great extent based on the ecash protocol of Schoenmakers [19] without using such trust relations. In addition, a bank issuing a universal currency does not underly the same infrastructural constraints as our coffee shop.

A recently proposed loyalty points protocol is given in [4]. It has a special focus on customer privacy in that it allows customers to build and reveal their own generalized profiles from their purchase history with the idea to award more loyalty points for more precise customer profiles. Customers therefore control their own degree of privacy. This protocol requires bilinear pairing based cryptography to implement its flexible customer privacy features, whereas PrivatePoints offers only basic customer privacy protection in return for a greatly reduced complexity of the system and cryptographic primitives used. In addition, this protocol is aimed at larger online and offline shops with a global taxonomy of products and makes explicit use of a certification agency.

Electronic customer loyalty systems are also related to coupon and voucher systems. The coupon systems most relevant to our work are [5,7,10,11]; the multi-coupon system described in [5] has the closest resemblance to the PrivatePoints protocol. The major difference lies in the use of cryptographic tools in that [5] uses proofs of knowledge, while PrivatePoints employs digital signature and commitment schemes. Moreover, loyalty points systems have stronger implementation requirements than voucher systems, since issuing loyalty points is an integral part of every transaction.

7 Conclusion and Future Work

We have illustrated the use of *communication topologies* to guide the design of security protocols. A communication topology is a graphical tool to represent assumptions about the environment that a protocol runs in. This guided approach to designing protocols does not guarantee secure protocols. For such guarantees, pen and paper proofs or automated verification tools are still required. Nevertheless, our approach helps in reducing the search space and can be used to sketch security protocol designs without the need for a deep understanding of the intricate details of formal security specifications.

An ulterior motive for our work is the question how secure protocols could be designed automatically. We envision the communication topologies to be one of the inputs that a user can conveniently specify in a graphical environment. The other input are the security requirements that are selected from a list. The envisioned automatic tool's first step is to find possible protocol flows in a similar manner as we have found manually in Sect. 3. The second step is to refine the protocol flows heuristically or interactively into protocol specifications that are in turn analyzed with a theorem prover or model checking tool.

The security protocols exemplarily designed in this paper using communication topologies are digital analogues of a paper-based customer loyalty program. They have been geared towards use in small shops with no professional or third-party-provided infrastructure available. In fact, we showed that our PrivatePoints protocol could even be used by an ice cream vendor in a football stadium using his private mobile phone for issuing and redemption of loyalty points. The implemented prototype protocol has been argued to offer the same security features as its paper-based ancestor, namely unforgeability of points, double-spending protection, theft protection of points, non-repudiation by the vendor, customer anonymity and customer privacy. The protocol does not require the customer's mobile device to be connected to the Internet and it is scalable enough to support point-per-product-purchased as well as point-per-euro-spent loyalty programs.

Concerning future work, we will investigate to which extent such a simple and light-weight loyalty point system can support collaborating shops and franchising companies that expect loyalty points issued in one shop to be redeemable in other shops. Especially in franchising companies, the individual shops may be competitors, which puts the straightforward idea of key sharing between shops into question.

References

1. Abadi, M., Needham, R.M.: Prudent engineering practice for cryptographic protocols. IEEE Trans. Softw. Eng. **22**(1), 6–15 (1996)
2. ECB (European Central Bank). Virtual currency schemes, October 2012
3. Basin, D., Radomirović, S., Schläpfer, M.: A complete characterization of secure human-server communication. In: 28th IEEE Computer Security Foundations Symposium (CSF 2015), pp. 199–213. IEEE Computer Society (2015). http://www.infsec.ethz.ch/research/projects/hisp.html

4. Blanco-Justicia, A., Domingo-Ferrer, J.: Privacy-preserving loyalty programs (2014). CoRR, abs/1411.3961

5. Canard, S., Gouget, A., Hufschmitt, E.: A handy multi-coupon system. In: Zhou, J., Yung, M., Bao, F. (eds.) ACNS 2006. LNCS, vol. 3989, pp. 66–81. Springer, Heidelberg (2006)

6. Chaum, D.: Blind signatures for untraceable payments. In: Chaum, D., Rivest, R.L., Sherman, A.T. (eds.) Advances in Cryptology, pp. 199–203. Springer, New York (1983)

7. Chen, L., Enzmann, M., Sadeghi, A.-R., Schneider, M., Steiner, M.: A privacy-protecting coupon system. In: S. Patrick, A., Yung, M. (eds.) FC 2005. LNCS, vol. 3570, pp. 93–108. Springer, Heidelberg (2005)

8. Cuennet, L.: Security protocols for loyalty card systems on mobile devices. Master's thesis, University Of Fribourg (2014)

9. Cumby, C., Fano, A., Ghani, R., Krema, M.: Predicting customer shopping lists from point-of-sale purchase data. In: Proceedings of the Tenth ACM SIGKDD International Conference on Knowledge Discovery and Data Mining, pp. 402–409. ACM (2004)

10. Dominikus, S., Aignerc, M.: mCoupons: an application for near field communication (NFC). In: 2007 21st International Conference on Advanced Information Networking and Applications Workshops, AINAW 2007, vol. 2, pp. 421–428. IEEE (2007)

11. Enzmann, M., Fischlin, M., Schneider, M.: A privacy-friendly loyalty system based on discrete logarithms over elliptic curves. In: Juels, A. (ed.) FC 2004. LNCS, vol. 3110, pp. 24–38. Springer, Heidelberg (2004)

12. Maurer, U.M., Schmid, P.E.: A calculus for secure channel establishment in open networks. In: Gollmann, D. (ed.) ESORICS 1994. LNCS, vol. 875, pp. 173–192. Springer, Heidelberg (1994)

13. Meier, S., Schmidt, B., Cremers, C., Basin, D.: The TAMARIN prover for the symbolic analysis of security protocols. In: Sharygina, N., Veith, H. (eds.) CAV 2013. LNCS, vol. 8044, pp. 696–701. Springer, Heidelberg (2013)

14. Pfitzmann, B., Waidner, M.: Properties of payment systems: general definiton sketch and classification (1996)

15. Quaresma, J.: On building secure communication systems. Ph.D. thesis, DTU Compute, Technical University of Denmark (2013)

16. Quaresma, J., Probst, C.W., Nielson, F.: The guided system development framework: modeling and verifying communication systems. In: Margaria, T., Steffen, B. (eds.) ISoLA 2014, Part II. LNCS, vol. 8803, pp. 509–523. Springer, Heidelberg (2014)

17. Radomirović, S.: Tamarin specification files for two loyalty points protocols (2015). http://www.infsec.ethz.ch/research/projects/hisp.html

18. Sadeghi, A.-R., Schneider, M.: Electronic payment systems. In: Becker, E., Buhse, W., Günnewig, D., Rump, N. (eds.) Digital Rights Management. LNCS, vol. 2770, pp. 113–137. Springer, Heidelberg (2003)

19. Schoenmakers, B.: Basic security of the ecash payment system. In: Preneel, B., Rijmen, V. (eds.) Computer Security and Industrial Cryptography: State of the Art and Evolution, pp. 342–356. Springer Verlag, New York (1998)

20. Song, D., Perrig, A., Phan, D.: AGVI - automatic generation, verification, and implementation of security protocols. In: Berry, G., Comon, H., Finkel, A. (eds.) CAV 2001. LNCS, vol. 2102, pp. 241–245. Springer, Heidelberg (2001)

21. Sprankel, S: Technical basis of digital currencies (2013)

22. Sprenger, C., Basin, D.: Developing security protocols by refinement. In: 7th ACM Conference on Computer and Communications Security (CCS 2010), 4–8 October 2010, Chicago, USA, pp. 361–374. ACM (2010)
23. von Solms, S., Naccache, D.: On blind signatures and perfect crimes. Comput. Secur. **11**, 581–583 (1992)

Transforming Graphical System Models to Graphical Attack Models

Marieta Georgieva Ivanova[1], Christian W. Probst[1(✉)], René Rydhof Hansen[2], and Florian Kammüller[3]

[1] Technical University of Denmark, Kongens Lyngby, Denmark
{mgiv,cwpr}@dtu.dk
[2] Aalborg University, Aalborg, Denmark
rrh@cs.aau.dk
[3] Middlesex University, London, UK
f.kammueller@mdx.ac.uk

Abstract. Manually identifying possible attacks on an organisation is a complex undertaking; many different factors must be considered, and the resulting attack scenarios can be complex and hard to maintain as the organisation changes. System models provide a systematic representation of organisations that helps in structuring attack identification and can integrate physical, virtual, and social components. These models form a solid basis for guiding the manual identification of attack scenarios. Their main benefit, however, is in the analytic generation of attacks. In this work we present a systematic approach to transforming graphical system models to graphical attack models in the form of attack trees. Based on an asset in the model, our transformations result in an attack tree that represents attacks by all possible actors in the model, after which the actor in question has obtained the asset.

1 Introduction

Organisations face a constant stream of attacks on their IT-infrastructure. Many of these attacks and the ways to prevent them are well understood. Traditional and well-established risk assessment methods can often identify these potential threats, but due to a technical focus, these approaches often abstract away the internal structure of an organisation and ignore human factors when modelling and assessing attacks. However, an increasing number of attacks do involve attack steps such as social engineering.

Attack trees [1,2] are a loosely defined, yet (or maybe therefore) widely used approach for documenting possible attacks in risk assessment [3]; they can describe attack goals and different ways of achieving these goals by means of the individual steps in an attack. The goal of the defender is then to inhibit one or more of the attack steps, thereby prohibiting the overall attack, or at least making it more difficult or expensive. While attacks trees for purely technical attacks may be constructed by automated means [4,5], for example by scanning networks and identifying software versions, this is currently not possible for

S. Mauw et al. (Eds.): GraMSec 2015, LNCS 9390, pp. 82–96, 2016.
DOI: 10.1007/978-3-319-29968-6_6

attacks exploiting the human factors. Actually, only few, if any, approaches to systematic risk assessment take such "human factor"-based attacks into consideration. The goal of the TRE$_S$PASS project [6] is to close this gap by developing models and analytic processes that support risk assessment in complex organisations including human factors and physical infrastructure. The goal of this support is to simplify the identification of possible attacks and to provide qualified assessment and ranking of attacks based on the expected impact.

In this work we present the fundamental approach to systematically transform graphical system models to graphical attack models in the form of attack trees. Since the transformation considers all relevant system components, the resulting attacks may include elements of human behaviour. These attacks can then be used as input to a traditional risk assessment process and thereby extend and support the brainstorming results. Our approach is applicable to a class of recent system models such as ExASyM [7] and Portunes [8], which have been used to model and analyse organisations for possible attacks [9]. These models contain both the physical infrastructure and information on actors, access rights, and policies; consequently, analysis of such models can include, for example, social engineering in the identified attacks.

The benefit of converting system models to attack models is a conceptually new view on qualitative security properties. The system model represents spatial connections on the different layers of an organisation, thus blurring potential attacks exploiting items not connected in the model, or not connected in the mental image of the modeller. Attack models represent connections between elements and actions that can be exploited to perform an attack.

Our transformations are independent of the underlying model. While we present them in the setting of the TRE$_S$PASS model, the general approach can be applied to any graphical system model. The transformations described in this work can be used as the core technique for policy invalidation [10,11], where policies describe both access control to locations and data, as well as system-wide policies such as admissible actions and actor behaviour. We have implemented the transformations presented in this work in an attack tree generator for TRE$_S$PASS models. The example shown in Fig. 9 has been generated with this tool.

The rest of this article is structured as follows. The next section gives an overview of graphical models for systems and attacks, followed by a description of the transformations for simple models in Sect. 3. These simple models do not consider mobility of data or other actors than the attacker. Mobility of data through processes is added in Sect. 4. Finally, Sect. 5 concludes the paper and discusses future work.

2   Graphical System Models and Attack Models

We start by introducing the main concepts in the system model and the attack models we consider. System models includes representations of both the physical and the digital infrastructure of an organisation. This is similar to approaches such as ExASyM [7] and Portunes [8], which represent relevant elements as nodes in a graph, that form the natural basis for the application of our techniques. However, for the current work, we do not require a particular kind of representation: the only requirement is that the core concepts discussed later in this section can be extracted from the underlying model. Similarly, attack models represent possible attacks on the modelled organisation. For the approach in this paper, we essentially only require that attack goals can be divided into sub-goals that can be combined either *conjunctively* (must all be completed) or *disjunctively* (only one sub-goal need to be completed). This is very similar to attack trees [1,2], and just as for these it would be interesting to allow more complex combinations at a later point.

2.1   Graphical System Models

We consider *nodes* as the central element in our graphical model of an organisation. We differentiate between nodes representing

- **Locations** in the organisation, for example, rooms, access control points, network components, computers, etc. Nodes representing locations that are physically or logically connected in the organisation, are linked by directed edges in the graph.
- **Actors** in the modelled organisation.
- **Processes** modelling information sharing or policies.
- **Items** modelling tangible assets in the modelled organisation, for example, access cards, harddrives, etc.

Additionally, nodes can store *items* and *data*; in contrast to items, that are represented by nodes, data is represented by an (abstract) name and includes, *e.g.*, pins, passwords, and other intangible assets. All elements in the model provide a unique identifier that can be used to refer to the element and to obtain, for example, information on its concrete type, model, or other relevant properties.

A location in the modelled organisation may belong to several *domains*, *e.g.*, it can be (physically) part of the building and also be present (virtually) on the network. Nodes in the model can also belong to different domains, which limit the operations that can be performed on a node and limiting where processes can move; human actors, for example, are restricted to nodes in the physical domain, and computer processes are restricted to nodes in the virtual domain.

Assets are used for modelling any kind of item or data that is relevant in the modelled organisation. In addition, assets can be annotated with extra information, *e.g.*, a probability representing how likely it is to lose a particular piece of data.

Nodes that represent processes or actors can *move* around in the model, *i.e.*, be associated to changing locations; actors are allowed to store both items and data, while processes can only store data. Assets stored at either of these nodes move around with the node.

To represent a wide variety of processes and the possible behaviour of actors, we assume that a number of simple **actions** can be performed on a target, which can be any location in the model, including physical locations or actors.

To constrain mobility of processes and actors, as well as to constrain actions, we assume a policy mechanism in the model, consisting of

- **Policies** that regulate access to locations and assets. Policies consist of required credentials and enabled actions, representing what an actor needs to provide in order to enable the actions in a policy, and what actions are enabled if an actor provides the required credentials, respectively.
- **Credentials** are data, items, or an identity that the actor or process performing an action needs to have, or predicates.

Predicates as credentials express that the actor must possess a certain attribute. In the example shown in Fig. 1, an actor must be trusted by Alice in order to be allowed to move to the location *Door*. We also assume policies to support variables to relate credentials to each other, or to restrict actions based on the credentials provided. In the example shown in Fig. 1, the policy at the ATM requires the actor to present a card with a pin X and the matching pin.

As stated above, both the ExASyM [7] and Portunes [8] modelling languages fulfil the above requirements for using our approach, as does any Klaim-like models [12] in general. While Klaim models process mobility by processes moving from node to node, we request processes to reside in special nodes that move around with the process. We choose this abstraction to make the modelling of (movement of) actors and assets carried by actors more intuitive and natural; mapping "standard" Klaim-like models to this abstraction is straightforward. In Fig. 1, for example, the node representing the actor Alice has a pin code and a card. The card in turn contains information about the owner and the pin code for the card.

In the work described here, we only consider the pure transformation of graphical system models to graphical attack models. An essential next step in risk assessment is to valuate the risk and impact of an attack, for example, by annotating the attack model with metrics and performing analyses on them [13]. This mapping can be achieved by associating the elements' identifiers with relevant metrics. These metrics can represent any quantitative knowledge about components, for example, likelihood, time, price, impact, or probability distributions. The latter could describe behaviour of actors or timing distributions. For the transformation described in this article these metrics are irrelevant, but they can be evaluated on the generated attack trees.

Containment. Items as described above are an important concept in our abstract model, since they can represent containment. Containment represents for example the fact that a workstation contains a harddrive that contains a file. In the model underlying our transformations we would represent the workstation as an item with a location; this location in turn would contain an item representing the harddrive; this item's location would contain data representing the (intangible) file.

We interpret containment as being transitive: if item a contains item b, and item b contains the data d, then we say a contains d transitively, and b contains d directly.

2.2 Graphical Attack Model

Attack trees [1,2] are widely used by various security analysis techniques; they support an easily accessible tree-like structure that can be visualised and understood by non-experts. At the same time, they can be subjected to formal analysis and structured treatment due to their tree-structure. Even though standard attack trees represent sub-goals that must be completed in a specific sequence, they have a hierarchical structure: the root node represents the attacker's goal, which is further refined by defining sub-goals. As mentioned above, the sub-goals can be represented as sub-trees in the overall attack tree, where sub-trees, *i.e.*, sub-goals, are combined conjunctively or disjunctively.

We do not require any further properties for the target of our transformations. In principle the transformation could embed additional information into the attack tree; for example, we currently assume an implicit left to right order in sub-goals of conjunctive nodes.

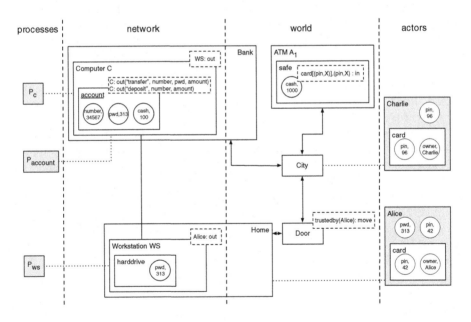

Fig. 1. Graphical representation of the example system. The white rectangles represent locations or items, the gray rectangles represent processes and actors; actors contain the items or data owned by the actor. The round nodes represent data. Solid lines represent the physical connections between locations, and dotted lines represent the present location of actors and processes. The dashed rectangles in the upper right part of some nodes represent the policies assigned to these nodes.

2.3 Running Example

The running example in this paper is based on a case study in the TRE$_S$PASS project [6] based on an actor Alice, who receives some kind of service, *e.g.*, care-taking, provided by an actor Charlie. Charlie's employer has a company policy that forbids him to accept money from Alice. Figure 1 shows a graphical representation of the example scenario, consisting of Alice's home, a bank with an ATM, and a bank computer. Alice owns a card and a concomitant pin code to obtain money from an ATM, and a password to initiate transfers from her workstation via the bank computer. Some of the nodes are labelled with policies in dashed boxes; for example the money at the ATM requires a card with a pin code, as well as that very pin code in order to obtain money (modelled as input).

Figure 1 shows a graphical representation of the model of our running example. The locations, represented by small rectangles, are connected through directed edges. Actors are represented as rectangles with a location, *e.g.*, Alice is at home and Charlie is in the city. Both actor nodes and location nodes can contain data and items represented as circles. In our example, Alice has a card that contains a pin code and Alice also has (knows) the pin code for her card. Actor nodes can also represent processes running on the corresponding locations. The processes at the workstation and the bank computer represent the required functionality for transferring money; they initiate transfers from Alice's home (P_{WS}), and check credentials for transfers (P_C).

3 Transforming Models Without Asset Mobility

The class of attacks we generate from graphical system models address attackers trying to reach a certain location or to obtain an asset. We mainly deal with confidentiality and integrity properties. We are currently working on extending this class to include attacks that aim at, *e.g.*, starting a process as part of a distributed denial-of-service attack. We expect to be able to generate these attacks with similar transformations. In this section we consider assets in the modelled organisation to be immobile. This restriction, which will be lifted in the next section, simplifies the first presentation of transformations.

Attack generation assumes an asset in the system, which an attacker should not be able to obtain. For every possible actor in the system, the goal of the transformation is then to generate an attack that results in the actor having obtained this asset. The overall transformation is a generalised version of policy invalidation [10,11]:

1. Starting from the goal asset and the attacking actor,
2. the transformation identifies all paths to the asset,
3. and for every path, identifies the credentials that the actor is lacking;
4. for each missing credential, a new transformation is started recursively;
5. after obtaining all necessary credentials, the actor can reach the location of the goal asset, and perform an action to obtain it.

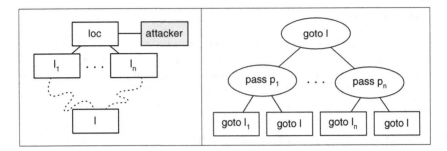

Fig. 2. Transforming a location. Any credential c_i that the attacker is lacking is obtained before performing action a at the location *loc*.

In the following, we present for each of the model elements discussed in the previous section, how they are transformed into an attack representation. For each transformation we show the part of the system model that triggers the translation as well as the generated part of the attack model. For the system models we use the same graphical representation as shown in Sect. 2.3 and Fig. 1. For attack models we use a special notation that represents parts of the attack as circles, and invocations of the transformation as rectangles.

3.1 Locations

A location is transformed into a disjunction of all possible paths from the locations already reached by the attacker to the location in question. Whenever traversing a path requires new credentials due to some policy, we recursively invoke the attack transformation, which ensures that the attacker obtains the necessary credentials to pass the path.

The transformation pattern is shown in Fig. 2. For every possible path we first generate one step to the first node of the path, followed by a recursive invocation of the transformation for going to the target location.

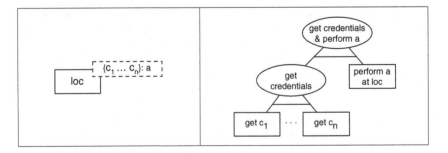

Fig. 3. Transforming a policy. If the attacker lacks any credential to perform action a at the location *loc*, the transformation creates an attack that obtains that credential.

3.2 Policies

If the transformation at any point needs to create an action that is prohibited by a policy, for which the attacker does not have all credentials, a new transformation is started to obtain this credential, resulting in a new attack representation. The transformation pattern is shown in Fig. 3.

As mentioned above, many system models support predicates as credentials, for example, to express that the actor must possess a certain attribute. In the example shown in Fig. 1, an actor must be trusted by Alice in order to be allowed to move to the location *Door*. Often, such a predicate is not a credential that can be obtained, as for trust. In this case, the transformation generates a social engineering action to "obtain" the predicate in question.

The variables in policies can be factored out before performing this transformation by identifying all sets of assets that fullfil a policy. For the example shown in Fig. 1 and the location ATM, the possible sets of assets are the card and the pin at Alice or at Charlie.

In the following we assume that the transformation generates all necessary steps for obtaining assets before performing the transformations described. In the resulting attack representation, the root node of the attack representation for obtaining the necessary credentials will be to the left of the root node for performing the following actions, expressing an ordering as described above.

3.3 Data

Data represents intangible assets, such as passwords or pins. For obtaining data, a conjunction is generated where the first element is to reach the location of the data (Fig. 4). Once the attacker has reached a location that contains the goal data, an action in the attack representation will be generated (Fig. 5) that depends on the kind of location that contains the data (Figs. 6, 7, 8):

– If the data is contained in a location, then a simple in action will be generated; or
– If the data is contained at an actor, then a social engineering action will be generated.

If the goal data is contained in an item i, the transformation generates the conjunction of several actions:

– Obtain the item and then obtain the data from the item; or
– Obtain the data from the item directly.

The difference between the two options is that the first option represents the case that the attacker obtains the containing item itself and then obtains the data, while the second option represents the case that the attacker removes the data or item in place.

For the example of the workstation mentioned before this would mean that the attacker either steals the harddrive containing the file, or that he extracts the file from the harddrive.

Fig. 4. Items and data may be available from different locations. For each of these locations, the transformation generates a separate attack path to obtain the asset. The transformation will generate attacks to obtain all necessary credentials, and then input the asset.

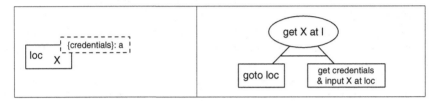

Fig. 5. To obtain an asset from a location, the transformation generates the necessary attack to go to the asset's location, then obtains the credentials, and finally performs the necessary **in** action.

3.4 Items

Items represent tangible assets, such as the aforementioned workstation, harddisk, or an access card. Just as for data, we generate a conjunction that first contains a node that represents reaching the location of an item (Fig. 4). Once the attacker has reached a location that contains the goal item, an action in the attack representation will be generated (Fig. 5) that depends on the kind of location that contains the item (Figs. 6, 7, 8):

– If the item is contained in a location, then a simple **in** action will be generated;
– If the item is contained at an actor, then a disjunction of a social engineering action or an **in** action will be generated, where the latter represents an attempt of stealing the item.

If the goal item is contained in another item, the transformation generates the conjunction of several actions:

– Obtain the item and then obtain the goal item from the item; or
– Obtain the goal item from the item directly.

The difference between the two options in the generated disjunctions is that the first option represents the case that the attacker obtains the containing item itself, while the second option represents the case that the attacker removes the data or item in place.

    For the example of the workstation mentioned before this would mean that the attacker either steals the workstation containing the harddrive, or that he extracts the harddrive from the workstation.

Fig. 6. To obtain an asset that is directly contained at a location, the transformation simply generates an **in** action. Note that the necessary credentials have been obtained before invoking this transformation.

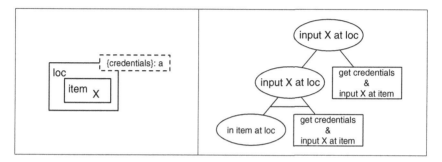

Fig. 7. To obtain an asset that is transitively contained at a location, the transformation first obtains the item containing the asset and then recursively invokes the transformation.

Fig. 8. Obtaining an asset from an actor is almost the same as for locations; the only difference is that assets can be obtained by social engineering. The transformation generates a special social engineering action, which is not further defined. Refining this action depends on the context of the action such as, *e.g.*, the involved actors; this is left to later phases that consume the generated attack.

3.5 Triggering the Transformation

In general the transformation will be triggered by a certain asset being off-limit for an attacker. The transformation iterates over a specified set of actors available in the system model, and generates for each of these actors all possible attacks for how they can obtain the asset. The triggering transformation for an asset X is $\boxed{\text{get } X}$. While transforming the system model into an attack model,

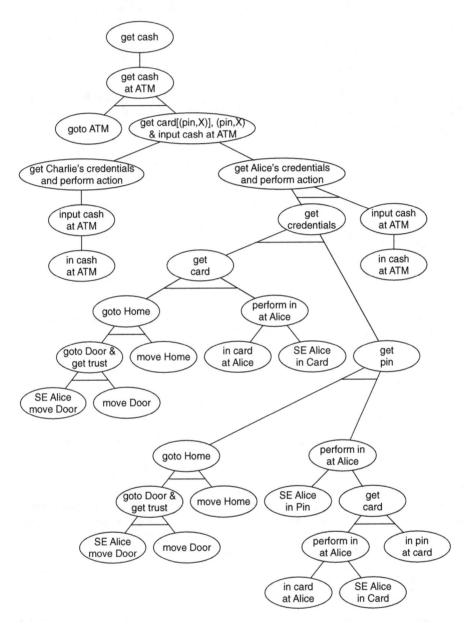

Fig. 9. Result of transforming the example from Fig. 1 using *cash* as the goal asset and Charlie as an attacker.

the transformation keeps track of the attacker, the location reached, and the assets obtained. The attacker may already possess assets before starting the transformation; this is specified in the system model.

3.6   Transforming the Example

We will now sketch the transformation of the example system discussed in Sect. 2.3 and shown in Fig. 1. We assume that the goal asset of the attacker is *cash*, which is available from locations *ATM A1* and *Computer*. We will only described data mobility in the next section, so for now we concentrate on the "physical" cash available at the ATM location.

As discussed above, the transformation considers all possible actors and starts with the $\boxed{\text{get } cash}$ action, which in turn will result in a $\boxed{\text{get } cash \text{ at } ATM}$ transformation (Fig. 4). This results in a conjunction of going to the ATM, getting the credentials, and inputting the asset at that location, since the goal asset is directly contained in the ATM.

The credentials at the *cash* asset require a card with a matching pin. In the example system, both Charlie and Alice own matching assets, so the transformation generates two possible attacks, one using Charlie's card, another using Alice's card. Clearly, the first transformation result does not necessarily represent an attack; generating such unwanted artefacts can either prohibited by restricting permissible actors in the policy,[1] or it can be dealt with in later phases that work on the generated attacks.

For the first possible attack, Charlie would use his own card and pin; this does not require further credentials. For the second possible attack, Charlie needs to obtain the pin and the card from Alice. Alice's location is *Home*, and to pass the path to this location, Charlie must fullfil the predicate *trustedby(Alice)*. This results in an action *social engineer Alice move Door*, which could in a later phase, for example, be translated into a forceful entrance or pretending to be somebody who Alice trusts or is likely to let in her home. Once the location *Home* has been reached, Charlie has several options for obtaining the card and the pin:

– Social Engineer Alice to give him the card and the pin;
– Input card from Alice (stealing); and
– Input the pin from the card (skimming).

The generated attack takes account for all combinations hereof; some parts of the tree can be pruned or simplified in a later phase similar to [4]. Once the card and the pin have been obtained, Charlie moves to the location *ATM* and inputs the asset *cash*.

The resulting attack model is shown in Fig. 9. Not surprisingly, the transformation result contains identical sub-trees due to identical assets to obtain or identical patterns being transformed. Similar to the actions for obtaining items, these could be simplified by a followup pass.

---

[1] In this case, the owner of the card would not be allowed to be the actor performing the action.

4 Adding Data Mobility

So far we have assumed assets to be at static locations. This assumption simplifies both the transformations for attack generation and the structure of the generated attacks; instead of having to consider all the locations that an asset can reach by means of actors or processes, we only have to consider the locations where data is available in the model. We now discuss how to loosen this restriction.

In Sects. 3.3 and 3.4 the transformations described assume that the data is available from a number of locations in the model, either directly or transitively. The main transformation starting the generation of sub-attacks is shown in Fig. 4. When adding data mobility, we are interested in which *other* locations the assets are able to reach, either by means of processes (for virtual assets) or by means of actors (for real-world assets).

The transformation for data mobility works reverse to the transformations we have presented in the previous section. Before being able to generate an attack, we need to perform three steps:

1. Identify who is able to move the asset;
2. Identify how to trigger the movement; and
3. Identify which locations the asset can reach.

The result of these steps is an attack that triggers the movement, and a set of locations that the asset can reach; these locations can then be used as input to the transformation shown in Fig. 4.

The main task lies in identifying who can trigger the movement and how. Beyond these steps, adding data mobility does not add to the transformation, but to the complexity of the generated attack model.

5 Conclusion

In this article we have presented a systematic approach for transforming graphic system models into graphical attack models. Graphical models in general have the advantage of easing understanding by non-technical personelle. This is a significant advantage especially when communicating the risk of attacks on an organisation. While the techniques discussed in this work especially target IT security attacks, the techniques are applicable to any kind of attacks and risks. Especially the support for social engineering attacks, though only at a very abstract level, enables handling of a wide class of attacks involving physical, virtual, and social layers of organisations. As recent events have shown, this class of attacks will become ever more important.

Our techniques help identifying and communicating attacks faced by organisation by enhancing traditional risk assessment methods that often abstract away the internal structure of an organisation and ignore human factors when modelling and assessing attacks. The attacks we identify consider all relevant system components, including elements of human behaviour, and can be used as input to a traditional risk assessment process.

Our approach is generally applicable to graphical system models and graphical attack models; examples for instances of such models include system models, *e.g.*, ExASyM [7] and Portunes [8], and attack models such as attack trees and attack-defence trees [1,2].

As discussed in Sect. 3, we are currently working on extending the class of generated attacks to include attacks that aim at, *e.g.*, starting a process as part of a distributed denial-of-service attack. Another extension of our approach aims at considering the environment in which the system under attack is used. This environment influences, *e.g.*, the value of data or assets, either for the organisation or the attacker. Finally, we are exploring the relation of our approach to transformations of UMLsec models to sequence diagrams representing attacks [14].

Acknowledgments. Part of the research leading to these results has received funding from the European Union Seventh Framework Programme (FP7/2007–2013) under grant agreement no. 318003 (TRE$_\text{S}$PASS). This publication reflects only the authors' views and the Union is not liable for any use that may be made of the information contained herein.

References

1. Schneier, B.: Attack trees: modeling security threats. Dr. Dobb's J. Softw. Tools **24**(12), 21–29 (1999)
2. Kordy, B., Piètre-Cambacédès, L., Schweitzer, P.: Dag-based attack and defense modeling: don't miss the forest for the attack trees. Comput. Sci. Rev. **13–14**, 1–38 (2014)
3. Pinchinat, S., Acher, M., Vojtisek, D.: Towards synthesis of attack trees for supporting computer-aided risk analysis. In: Canal, C., Idani, A. (eds.) SEFM 2014 Workshops. LNCS, vol. 8938, pp. 363–375. Springer, Heidelberg (2015)
4. Vigo, R., Nielson, F., Nielson, H.R.: Automated generation of attack trees. In: Proceedings of the 27th Computer Security Foundations Symposium (CSF), pp. 337–350. IEEE (2014)
5. Hong, J.B., Kim, D.S., Takaoka, T.: Scalable attack representation model using logic reduction techniques. In: Proceedings of the 12th IEEE International Conference on Trust, Security and Privacy in Computing and Communications (TrustCom), pp. 404–411, July 2013
6. The Consortium: Project web page. http://www.trespass-project.eu
7. Probst, C.W., Hansen, R.R.: An extensible analysable system model. Inf. Secur. Tech. Rep. **13**(4), 235–246 (2008)
8. Dimkov, T., Pieters, W., Hartel, P.: Portunes: representing attack scenarios spanning through the physical, digital and social domain. In: Armando, A., Lowe, G. (eds.) ARSPA-WITS 2010. LNCS, vol. 6186, pp. 112–129. Springer, Heidelberg (2010)
9. Probst, C.W., Hansen, R.R., Nielson, F.: Where can an insider attack? In: Dimitrakos, T., Martinelli, F., Ryan, P.Y.A., Schneider, S. (eds.) FAST 2006. LNCS, vol. 4691, pp. 127–142. Springer, Heidelberg (2007)

10. Kammüller, F., Probst, C.W.: Invalidating policies using structural information. In: Proceedings of the 2nd International IEEE Workshop on Research on Insider Threats (WRIT 2013). IEEE Co-located with IEEE CS Security and Privacy 2013 (2013)
11. Kammüller, F., Probst, C.W.: Combining generated data models with formal invalidation for insider threat analysis. In: Proceedings of the 3rd International IEEE Workshop on Research on Insider Threats (WRIT 2014). IEEE Co-located with IEEE CS Security and Privacy 2014 (2014)
12. de Nicola, R., Ferrari, G.L., Pugliese, R.: KLAIM: a kernel language for agents interaction and mobility. IEEE Trans. Softw. Eng. $\mathbf{24}$(5), 315–330 (1998)
13. Aslanyan, Z., Nielson, F.: Pareto efficient solutions of attack-defence trees. In: Focardi, R., Myers, A. (eds.) POST 2015. LNCS, vol. 9036, pp. 95–114. Springer, Heidelberg (2015)
14. Jürjens, J., Wimmel, G.: Security modelling for electronic commerce: The common electronic purse specifications. In: Towards The E-Society: E-Commerce, E-Business, and E-Government, The First IFIP Conference on E-Commerce, E-Business, E-Government (I3E 2001), pp. 489–505 (2001)

ATSyRa: An Integrated Environment for Synthesizing Attack Trees
(Tool Paper)

Sophie Pinchinat[✉], Mathieu Acher, and Didier Vojtisek

IRISA/Inria, Campus de Beaulieu, 35042 Rennes Cedex, France
{sophie.pinchinat,mathieu.acher,didier.vojtisek}@irisa.fr

Abstract. Attack trees are widely considered in the fields of security for the analysis of risks (or threats) against electronics, computer control, or physical systems. A major barrier is that attack trees can become largely complex and thus hard to specify. This paper presents ATSyRA, a tooling environment to automatically synthesize attack trees of a system under study. ATSyRA provides advanced editors to specify high-level descriptions of a system, high-level actions to structure the tree, and ways to interactively refine the synthesis. We illustrate how users can specify a military building, abstract and organize attacks, and eventually obtain a readable attack tree.

1 Introduction

Attack trees [8] provide a systematic way of describing the vulnerability of a system, taking various types of attacks into account. Strengths of attack trees rely on two aspects: they combine an intuitive representation of possible attacks with formal mathematical ways of analyzing them in a qualitative and quantitative way [4,6]. Kordy et al. showed that attack trees have been extensively studied by the scientific community and are widely considered within the industry [5].

Up to now, analysts and technicians usually construct attack trees manually, based on their knowledge and experience. A large number of tools for editing and analyzing attack trees exist (see, e.g., [3,4]). Unfortunately, the manual design of attack trees is time-consuming and error-prone, especially if the size of the attack tree becomes substantial. Moreover, a manual design is likely to be incomplete and unsound w.r.t. the security issues of a system under consideration. Supported by automation, practitioners can obtain large attack trees that are correct by construction and in line with the properties of the system. Moreover the generation process can also be reiterated in case new kinds of attacks emerge or the system evolves. As a consequence, automated generation of attack trees recently attracts the attention of researchers and industry practitioners [2,9,11,12].

Specifically, our long-term objective is to develop a (semi-)automated process, applicable to a large panel of risk analysis domains (physical security, communication security and dependability, business, management, engineering, etc.), that will assist practitioners in fulfilling the security modeling task. This paper

© Springer International Publishing Switzerland 2016
S. Mauw et al. (Eds.): GraMSec 2015, LNCS 9390, pp. 97–101, 2016.
DOI: 10.1007/978-3-319-29968-6_7

presents ATSyRA[1] a tool for synthesizing attack trees. ATSyRA is built upon the mathematical foundations presented in [7]. Compared to [2,9,11,12], ATSyRA aims to provide an interactive and user-guided synthesis; an integrated environment with domain-specific languages (DSLs) and advanced editors. We also aim to augment the level of abstraction and consider as input high-level description of a system for generating attack trees.

Remainder. Section 2 presents the underlying methodology. Section 3 illustrates the main features of ATSyRA. Section 4 identifies future work.

2   Towards Synthesis of Attack Trees

At the algorithmic level, we experienced that a naive fully automated generation is likely to produce unexploitable trees (because they are flat), as also noticed by [2]. Mauw and Oostdijk [6] and Kordy et al. [4] showed that numerous structurally different attacks trees can capture the same information, out of which a few are readable and meaningful for an expert. An original and crucial feature of our methodology is the support of *high-level actions (HLA)* [7] to specify how sequences of actions can be abstracted and structured – a high-level action can be seen as a sub-goal of the attacker.

The typical workflow is depicted in Fig. 1: inputs, either given by the practitioners or generated by the tool, are depicted in round-corner boxes (1)–(4), and intermediate tools/transformations are depicted in rectangle boxes (a)–(b). Dashed arrows suggest partial automation and an involvement of users to generate the results.

3   ATSyRa: Tooling the Approach

We implement an environment, called ATSyRA, for realizing the methodology previously introduced. Our experience for assessing the physical security of military buildings[2] motivated its design. The tool assists practitioners in synthesizing attack trees from the high-level description of the system. In our case, we develop a *domain-specific language (DSL)* for expressing military buildings. Other DSLs can be considered as well. ATSyRA[3] is implemented on top of Eclipse and offers to experts different facilities (DSLs' services like editors and automated reasoning support). Box (0) in Fig. 1 is a screen-shot of the ATSyRA environment, with windows ①-④, which we now detail.

① Experts define the system in a dedicated, textual or graphical language, called a Building specification, which is composed of three main parts: the *building description*, the attacker's *strength level*, and her *attack objective*.
  – The building description is entirely determined by a finite set of elements of four types: *zones* (rooms, garden, etc.), *accesses* (doors, windows, etc.), *items* (keys) and *alarms*. Each type of elements is equipped with an

---

[1] For "Attack-Tree Sythesis for Risk Analysis".

[2] In the context of a collaboration between IRISA and Defense Ministry in France (DGA).

[3] http://tinyurl.com/ATSyRA.

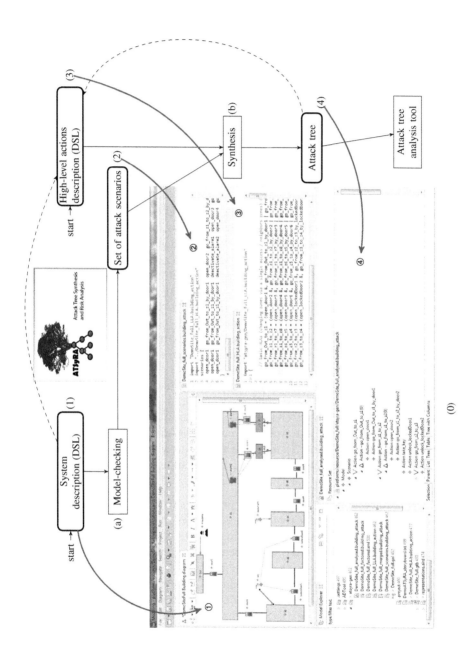

Fig. 1. The ATSyRA workflow

attribute, called its *defense level*, which determines the minimum strength attacker must possess in order to act on this very element.

- The attacker's strength level is modelled by an integer value, that denotes her knowledge and skills necessary to execute a given action on a given element (such as opening a door, or using a key). This choice is by no mean a definitive one, but it is acceptable for the first version of the tool.
- The attack objective consists of a final zone to reach, with some items collected, and determines whether the scenario may be subject to detection by alarms.

② Experts then run the generation of the set of attack scenarios. The underlying process is the compilation of the Building specification into an attack graph. The transitions of this attack graph are labelled by *(atomic) actions* inferred from the building's elements description, and which are executable by the attacker (according to her strength level). The compilation process is highly compositional, allowing for the generation of a symbolic (hence very succinct) attack graph. The target language is GAL (for "Guarded Action Language") [1], a simple yet expressive formalism to model concurrent systems which is supported by a very efficient decision diagram library for model-checking [10]. ATSyRA notably exploits a tuned reachability analysis procedure. The objective is to produce the sequences of atomic actions that yield paths in the graph and that correspond to winning attack scenarios.

③ Experts specify a set of high-level actions (HLAs) with a dedicated, textual language. An HLA is described in terms of how it can be refined into less abstract actions. The formalism is inspired from context-free grammars [7]: HLAs are the non-terminal symbols of the grammar, atomic actions are terminal symbols, and refinements are derivation rules.

④ Experts eventually run the attack tree synthesis: this "final" step exploits both HLAs specifications ③ and generated attack scenarios ②. It relies on bottom-up syntactic analysis techniques for the context-free derivation rules given by the HLAs and input words given by the attack scenarios. Then, an algorithm (see details in [7]) merges the syntactic trees into the attack tree, the nodes of which have type ranging over disjunction, conjunction and sequential conjunction.

ATSyRA is developed using model-driven principles technologies (e.g., Xtext, Sirius). We can deliver almost for free advanced editors, being textual or graphical, with auto-completion, syntax highlighting, location of errors, etc. Experts that specify military buildings or HLA thus benefit from advanced and dedicated editing support. Another benefit is that our model-based tool is extensible. Other inputs for the high-level description of a system can be seamlessly integrated and come with advanced editors as well. For instance we are investigating the use of system description languages (e.g., SySML) as part of ATSyRA.

4   Conclusion

We presented ATSyRA, an environment built on top of Eclipse, to support a methodology for synthesizing attack trees. Starting from a military building, we illustrated how security experts can specify high-level actions and eventually generate readable and well-structured attack trees.

As future work, we plan to consider other inputs – beyond military building specification – in other fields (e.g., computer networks). As the synthesis process is likely to be interactive and incremental, we plan to integrate as part of ATSyRA some visualisations and suggestions that can help an expert. We hope ATSyRA can be of interest for practitioners and researchers in charge of analyzing security risks with attack trees.

Acknowledgements. This work is funded by the Direction Générale de l'Armement (DGA) - Ministère de la Défense, France. We thank Salomé Coavoux and Maël Guilleme for their insightful comments and development around ATSyRA.

References

1. Colange, M., Baarir, S., Kordon, F., Thierry-Mieg, Y.: Towards distributed software model-checking using decision diagrams. In: Sharygina, N., Veith, H. (eds.) CAV 2013. LNCS, vol. 8044, pp. 830–845. Springer, Heidelberg (2013)
2. Hong, J.B., Kim, D.S., Takaoka, T.: Scalable attack representation model using logic reduction techniques. In: 12th IEEE International Conference on Trust, Security and Privacy in Computing and Communications, pp. 404–411 (2013)
3. Kordy, B., Kordy, P., Mauw, S., Schweitzer, P.: ADTool: security analysis with attack–defense trees. In: Joshi, K., Siegle, M., Stoelinga, M., D'Argenio, P.R. (eds.) QEST 2013. LNCS, vol. 8054, pp. 173–176. Springer, Heidelberg (2013)
4. Kordy, B., Mauw, S., Radomirović, S., Schweitzer, P.: Attack-defense trees. J. Log. Comput. **24**(1), 55–87 (2014)
5. Kordy, B., Piètre-Cambacédès, L., Schweitzer, P.: DAG-based attack and defense modeling: don't miss the forest for the attack trees. Comput. Sci. Rev. **13–14**, 1–38 (2014)
6. Mauw, S., Oostdijk, M.: Foundations of attack trees. In: Won, D.H., Kim, S. (eds.) ICISC 2005. LNCS, vol. 3935, pp. 186–198. Springer, Heidelberg (2006)
7. Pinchinat, S., Acher, M., Vojtisek, D.: Towards synthesis of attack trees for supporting computer-aided risk analysis. In: Canal, C., Idani, A. (eds.) SEFM 2014 Workshops. LNCS, vol. 8938, pp. 363–375. Springer, Heidelberg (2015)
8. Schneier, B.: Attack trees : modeling security threats. Dr. Dobb's J. **24**(12), 21–29 (1999)
9. Paul, S.: Towards automating the construction & maintenance of attack trees: a feasibility study. In: Kordy, B., Mauw, S., Pieters, W. (eds.) GraMSec, vol. 148, pp. 31–46. EPTCS (2014)
10. Thierry-Mieg, Y.: Symbolic model-checking using ITS-tools. In: Baier, C., Tinelli, C. (eds.) TACAS 2015. LNCS, vol. 9035, pp. 231–237. Springer, Heidelberg (2015)
11. TREsPASS: Technology-supported Risk Estimation by Predictive Assessment of Socio-technical Security, FP7 project, grant agreement 318003 (2012–2016). http://www.trespass-project.eu/
12. Vigo, R., Nielson, F., Nielson, H.R.: Automated generation of attack trees. In: 2014 IEEE 27th Computer Security Foundations Symposium (CSF), pp. 337–350. IEEE (2014)

Author Index

Printed in the United States
By Bookmasters